LEADERSHIP WITHOUT EXCUSES

LEADERSHIP WITHOUT EXCUSES

HOW TO CREATE ACCOUNTABILITY
AND HIGH PERFORMANCE
(INSTEAD OF JUST TALKING ABOUT IT)

JEFF GRIMSHAW
GREGG BARON

New York Chicago San Francisco Lisbon London
Madrid Mexico City Milan New Delhi San Juan
Seoul Singapore Sydney Toronto

1 2 3 4 5 6 7 8 9 0   DOC/DOC   1 5 4 3 2 1 0

ISBN: 978-0-07-160004-0
MHID: 0-07-160004-3

McGraw-Hill books are available at special quantity discounts to use as premiums and sales promotions, or for use in corporate training programs. To contact a representative please e-mail us at bulksales@mcgraw-hill.com.

This book is printed on acid-free paper.

To my parents, Richard and Charlotte, for their example. To Tanya, who holds me accountable for practicing what I preach.
—JG

To my wife, Nancy, for being an incredible partner; the team at Success Sciences for their dedication and talent; and to all of the clients we have been privileged to serve.
—GB

CONTENTS

CONTENTS

ACKNOWLEDGMENTS

Publishing conventions precluded us from putting a dozen or so names on the cover. That's unfortunate, as each member of our core team earned authorship credit for contributing original insights and content. That team of coauthors and contributors includes Lynne Viscio, Jan Lee, Barry Mike, Neill Edwards, Lilly Linton, and Alex Gwozda. Most of all, Tanya Mann and Ross Wilken deserve acknowledgment and our gratitude for their investment of blood, sweat, time, and brain power. More than half the chapters in the book directly reflect their insights.

Chris Thorsen, Kellie Hamrick, Amy Amundson, Josh Peskin, and Rebecca Cichetti also made essential contributions.

If we managed to express any original ideas in these pages, Emil Bohn is most likely their intellectual godfather.

We also owe a debt of gratitude to Laurie Spoon, Carolynne Bernard, Michelle McDermott, Jonathan Miller, Ariel Ptak, Kristen Senior, Jennifer Landis, Jean Cuce, John Cook, Suzanne Peterson, Alan Nelson, Joe Folger,

Megan Scala, Lani Van Dusen, Sandy Nelson, Will Sparks, Beverly Evans, Beverly Teague, Anne Murray-Randolph, Cindy Adams, Ronnie Chriss, Enitan Adesanya, Rick Ginley, Deborah Breines, Nicole Boscia, John McDermott, Michael A. Tysarczyk, Don P. Foster, Yvonne Cook, Roberta "Bert" Snow, Linda Heigh, Beverly Evans, Faith Drennan, Bethmarie Fahey, Ted and Mary Anne Regan, Barbara Greene, Emilie Hafner-Burton, David Viktor, Keith Coe, Greg Grimshaw, Jeremy Grimshaw, Anna M. Grimshaw, lots of other Grimshaws, Ted Edwards, Hillary Buckholtz, Catherine Hernandez, Karen Yolton, Mark Newman, Bob Kantor, Mike Grottola, Tobias Mayer, Susan Hazlett, John Brownfield, Hank Guenther, Denny Moutray, Duane Farrington, Rebecca Cohen, Andrea Coville, Walt Lockwood, Barbara Bauer, Harold Nelson, John Brodeur, and Dave Conti. Thanks also to Mal O'Connor and our friends at the Center for Applied Research (CFAR).

We can't forget the team at McGraw-Hill. Our first editor, Herb Schaffner, championed our cause, while Knox Huston, our second editor, ably guided us across the finish line. Both believed in us and helped bring out our best. Thanks also to Rik Kranenburg, Tom Stanton, Mary Skafides, Daina Penikas, and Ed Chupak.

Finally, for inspiring us to "live without excuses," we want to thank our friend Paul Pinkerton, a combat vet, rogue POW/MIA activist, cancer survivor, and humanitarian. Paul, in your honor, we'll donate a portion of the proceeds of *Leadership without Excuses* to Paul's Kids Vietnam Children's Charity.

INTRODUCTION

There are three kinds of people. What sets them apart is how much they're going to help you, their leader, deliver the business results on which you've staked your reputation.

Saints are *always* accountable. You can consistently rely on them to do the right things. To make smart choices. To follow through on commitments. To operate in compliance. And to do other things that are important to your organization's performance and survival. Maybe the saints do these things because they are fundamentally great people. Or maybe they're just the perfect fit—for the job, your team, and the organization. Regardless, saints make you look good as a leader (whether you deserve it or not). Unfortunately, saints comprise only a fraction of most organizations.

What do you do with saints? You don't want to lose them, so you reward and protect them. Vigilantly. What you can't do is give them more work to do to compensate for your failure to hold poor performers accountable. We'll say more about this in the coming pages. But we're not focused primarily on the topic of leading saints. (After all, if you were fortunate enough to have an all-saints workforce, it'd be unlikely you'd have felt motivated to open this book.)

Sinners are the opposite of saints. You can't count on them to do anything consistently except make excuses why they aren't delivering the performance and results you need. Maybe they're fundamentally bad people. Or just fundamentally bad hires. Either way, sinners reflect negatively on you as a leader (whether you deserve it or not). Fortunately, in most organizations, they too are usually small in number.

What do you do with sinners? Ideally, you don't hire them. This is why we're fans of rigorous hiring processes and probationary periods for new recruits to validate fit. Even then, you're still likely to end up with some sinners. So you have to get rid of them. Again, we'll say a bit more about this later on. But this book is not really focused on sinners either.

Instead, this book is focused primarily on leading the third kind of people: *save-ables*. Most people are save-ables. Sometimes they make good choices; sometimes they don't. They'll consistently do the right things, demonstrate accountability, deliver high performance, and give you what you need only under certain conditions. To create these conditions, you've got to understand and address their hardwired human frailties. There are three in particular you need to worry about. Specifically, the very predictable problems with the all-too-human save-ables are that (1) they can't read your mind, (2) they're

Figure I-1 Three Kinds of People and Their Typical Distribution.

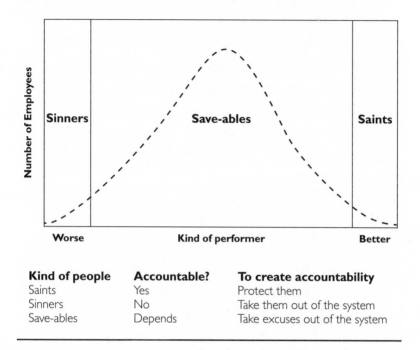

Kind of people	Accountable?	To create accountability
Saints	Yes	Protect them
Sinners	No	Take them out of the system
Save-ables	Depends	Take excuses out of the system

selfish, and (3) they're frequently delusional. Let's look briefly at each of these human frailty factors and how to address them (Figure I-1).

They Can't Read Minds

Your save-ables can't read your mind. So if you've not communicated *clear and credible expectations* for performance, you've effectively (albeit unintentionally) equipped them with an excuse for not doing what's needed.

The big insight here is that communicating clear and credible expectations is much harder than it sounds. It's not just something leaders should get around to after they've done their real work. "It *is* the work," says Len Schlesinger, president of Babson College and former chief operations officer (COO) of Limited Brands. "There's nothing particularly special about communicating expectations . . . other than all the things that tend to go wrong when people are 'too busy' to attend to it." For examples, check out "The Save-ables' Excuses" sidebar.

They're Selfish

When we say that save-ables are selfish, it doesn't mean that they're bad people. As the father of capitalism, Adam Smith, wrote in *The Wealth of Nations*, "It is not from the benevolence of the butcher, the brewer, or the baker that we expect our dinner, but from their regard to their own self-interest." The same principle applies to your save-ables: They won't do the right things because they're benevolent, but rather "in regard to their own self-interest."

This is why it's so important to create *compelling consequences*—aligned with the performance and behavior you need. If you are, as management professor Steve Kerr famously put it, "rewarding A while hoping for B," you've equipped your save-ables with a good excuse not to do what's needed. Because whatever you're rewarding and tolerating (intentionally or not), the save-ables are going to give you more of it. A big insight here—one that we'll elaborate on in the coming pages—is that you have a lot more power than you probably realize to create compelling consequences—both positive and negative—in order to motivate your save-ables to do the right things.

They're Frequently Delusional

Save-ables are prone to self-deception. But it's not their fault. Really. In *Welcome to Your Brain*,[1] neuroscientists Sandra Aamodt and Sam Wang explain that

> Your brain lies to you a lot. . . . For the most part, it's doing a great job, working hard to help you survive and accomplish your goals. . . . Because you often have to react quickly to emergencies and opportunities alike, your brain usually aims to get a [half-baked] answer in a hurry rather than a perfect answer that takes awhile to figure out. . . . [T]his means that your brain has to take shortcuts . . . [which] lead to predictable mistakes.

In other words, humans simply are not hardwired for honest self-assessment because it was not an evolutionary tool helpful for our survival as a species. The quick-triggered decision making and defensiveness that enabled our distant ancestors to fend off saber tooth tigers predisposes us to narcissistic self-deceptions and excuse making.

For example, a little self-deception can go a long way toward helping save-ables rationalize why they deserve credit for successes—or merely for good intentions—whereas mistakes and failures are not their fault. A dose of delusion also comes in handy when the goal is to produce an alibi ("Don't look at me. I didn't know anything about it."), justify a misstep ("I had no choice."), or minimize a broken commitment ("It's only two days late.") or its outcome ("They were a pain-in-the-butt client anyway. Good riddance to them.").[2]

To take away those excuses, and others like them, it's essential to lead *conversations grounded in empirical reality*. Empirical reality is the reality we verify with our senses. It refers to the way things really are, as opposed to the way we'd like them to be. If you are, as the philosopher William James put it, a "lover of facts," you're more likely to enjoy a comfortable working relationship with empirical reality (though more claim this affinity than practice it).

The big (if obvious) insight here is that when your people see you indulging in magical thinking, it licenses them to do the same. Accordingly, if you want your save-ables to get real, you've got to lead by example.

The Save-ables' Excuses

Typical comments we've heard when conducting Conditions of Accountability Assessments:

Failures to Communicate Clear and Credible Expectations

- They want us to get excited and engaged around our new "strategic direction." But it's just one of eight things in the past year they've asked us to get excited and engaged about.

- They always say "do the right thing," and we all believe in it. Then we hit a situation where we need an expensive replacement for a customer, but I need three layers of approval, one of whom is out for two weeks. The field is yelling at me: "We're gonna lose this client!" Telling me to "just do the right thing" doesn't provide a solution.

- We do a lot of "rock hunting." My boss sends me to look for a rock. When I come back, he says, "No, that's not the rock I was looking for." So I go looking for another rock, hoping I get luckier next time.

- We don't get anything done because no one can make a decision, but anyone can veto it.

Failures to Create Compelling Consequences (That Are Aligned with Desired Performance)

- They seem to have no idea what really motivates us. They never ask.

- They reward and recognize average performers the same way they reward high performers. So what's the point of killing myself and taking time away from my family in order to be a high performer?

- The people who create the most drama get the most attention. So now I know what to do if I want my boss to focus on me.
- We say we care about customer service, but all they measure and pay us for is productivity. So the people who are actually dumb enough to really care about the customers are penalized for it.
- The "reward" for high performers is getting more work to do, while the poor performers stand off to the side.
- They say they're going to get serious about holding people accountable, but they never do. They usually just promote or transfer poor performers to make them someone else's problem.

Failures to Lead Conversations Grounded in Empirical Reality

- We say we want openness and honesty. But that's just one of the lies we tell ourselves. I've seen them shoot too many messengers of bad news to believe it.
- Apparently, there was a problem with my performance, but I was the last one in the department to learn about it. No one gave me the feedback until my year-end review.

- They say they want more innovation. But if I come up with a smarter way of doing things, I'll need to get seven people to approve it first. I don't have that much energy.
- Everyone secretly knows this initiative is going to fail. But no one is willing to say it out loud.
- As a group, we claim credit for our successes but blame our failures on external factors.
- We never learn from our mistakes because that would require us to acknowledge them. So we just keep repeating them.

The Three Conditions of Accountability

Our research and experience tell us that if you consistently and effectively create the three *conditions of accountability* by

- Communicating clear and credible expectations
- Creating compelling consequences
- Leading conversations grounded in empirical reality

then your save-ables will consistently give you what you need. In fact, they will become nearly indistinguishable from your saints. And this makes the sinners very conspicuous and therefore easy to spot and cast from your midst (before they lead any save-ables in the wrong direction).

When you fail to create the conditions of accountability, though, you unintentionally equip your save-ables with excuses—sometimes very good ones—for not doing what you need them to do. Which makes sense. If your people don't know what to do, don't feel motivated to do it, and aren't having real conversations about it, no one should be surprised when they make bad choices and let you down.

And when this happens, you've put your own goals, reputation, and survival in jeopardy. On top of that, you've created a situation in which it's pretty difficult to distinguish between your save-ables and your sinners—in which case, you won't know who to fire.

Temptations

As we said earlier, most people are save-ables. Whether they are accountable has less to do with their inherent nature and more to do with the situational contexts in which they find themselves and, to be more precise, whether the three conditions of accountability are in place. But leaders face a powerful temptation to sort people who are really save-ables into one of the other two categories.

Giving Halos to People Who Don't Deserve Them

Sometimes leaders confer sainthood not on the basis of consistent performance but rather to individuals they like or to whom they otherwise feel emotionally connected. And then when these "saints" misbehave or fail to do the right things, the leader rationalizes the bad behavior or downplays its significance. The problem is the double standard. Having two standards of accountability—one for cronies and another for everyone else—jeopardizes leadership credibility, creates resentment, and undermines the effectiveness of all other efforts to take excuses out of the system.

Sodom and Gomorrah Fallacy

An even bigger problem is leaders lumping their save-ables in with their sinners without proper due diligence. We understand the temptation. Because taking excuses out of the system is so challenging, lots of leaders make excuses as to why it isn't worth the effort. "I don't want to put any effort into creating the conditions of accountability," they say, "because it won't do any good. I'm stuck with a bunch of sinners."

You might be thinking the same thing. And though it's possible that you're right, we think it's highly unlikely that your workforce, like the Old Testament's twin cities of Sodom and Gomorrah, consists almost entirely of fundamentally bad people. If this is really true, your human resources (HR) department (or whoever recruited them) should be destroyed, which is what God did to the inhabitants of Sodom and Gomorrah when Abraham couldn't find anyone righteous there. While HR is always an easy target of wrath, it's more likely that you as the leader are part of the problem! Sinners are the people who aren't doing what's needed *after* you've done your best to create the conditions of accountability. Until you do that, it's irresponsible to claim that you can distinguish them from your save-ables.

Leadership without Excuses

Again, we understand why its tempting to lump your save-ables in with sinners instead of trying harder to "save" them by more aggressively creating the conditions of accountability. As we've acknowledged, it's very hard work. This important responsibility is—or ought to be—why you take home the big bucks (and are worth every penny). And this is why we wrote this book: To make the task a little easier by equipping you with a few new practical insights that you can put to use immediately.

In the first section of the book we'll focus on powerful, proven leadership strategies for *communicating clear and credible expectations.* We hope the second section of this book will change the way you feel about *creating compelling consequences.* And the third section describes approaches to *leading conversations grounded in empirical reality.*

PROVEN STRATEGIES FOR COMMUNICATING CLEAR AND CREDIBLE EXPECTATIONS

- ✓ Equip your people for moments of truth and tradeoff (Chapter 1).
- ✓ Invest excruciating minutes to ensure role clarity (Chapter 2).
- ✓ Use commander's intent to promote ownership, stretch your people, and align them with your business strategy (Chapter 3).
- ✓ Compete for attention (Chapter 4).
- ✓ Boost the credibility of your high expectations (Chapter 5).

CHAPTER 1

EQUIP YOUR PEOPLE FOR MOMENTS OF TRUTH AND TRADEOFF

In a famous study[1] conducted some years ago at Princeton Theological Seminary, researchers recruited a group of young seminarians and prepared them to give a talk on the Parable of the Good Samaritan. In this parable, you may recall, a traveler on the road to Jericho is robbed and beaten by thieves who leave him half-dead. A priest comes, sees the beaten traveler, and passes by. And then an assistant priest does the same. Finally, a Samaritan arrives on the scene, bandages the man's wounds, brings him to an inn, and takes care of him.

After the researchers prepared the seminarians to give a talk on the story and its implications, they sent students off, one by one, to fulfill their assignment. Some were directed to move very quickly and told, "You're a few minutes late.

They were expecting you a few minutes ago." Members of the second, "medium hurry" group were told, "The assistant is ready. Please go right over." But there was no rush for the members of third group, who were told, "It will be a few minutes before they need you, but you might as well head on over."

On the way to their assignment, each seminarian encountered a man on the sidewalk, slumped over, coughing and moaning. Unbeknownst to the seminarians, this man was a confederate—an actor who was part of the experiment.

Of the seminarians instructed to rush to their assignment to talk about the Parable of the Good Samaritan, only 10 percent stopped to help the man. The others walked past him—or over him. The seminarians in the second group, who'd been told merely to "go right over," fared better: Nearly half of them stopped to help the man—but the other half did not. Meanwhile, a majority of the seminarians in the third group, who weren't in any rush, stopped on their way to *speaking* about the Good Samaritan to *act* like one.[2]

What's true of many of the seminarians in this study is also true of many employees in the organizations where we've worked. They know what it means to do the right thing. In fact, like the seminarians, they know it well enough that they can explain it to others, at least in theory. But when they encounter high-pressure "moments of truth and tradeoff" where "doing the right thing" and completing an assigned task (or otherwise "getting results" or pursuing other self-interests) seem to them mutually exclusive options, they often make the wrong choice. Part of the challenge is that most organizations do a lousy job of preparing their employees for these moments.

The Business Case for Doing the Right Thing

Preparing employees for moments of truth and tradeoff isn't just "the right thing to do." There's a solid business case for it. When you fail to do so, you equip them with excuses for engaging in behaviors that, in an instant, can put years of investment in your organization's reputational and financial assets at great risk. For proof, one need only to look at the mess that has taken out so many Wall Street firms and left even the strongest survivors with black eyes.

But covering your assets isn't the only reason. Productivity is another. When employees are spending lots of energy trying to divine what the organization *really* values, it distracts them from what you're paying them to do. That's attention they aren't investing in solving problems and getting results.

Some years ago the chief executive officer (CEO) and chief operations officer (COO) of one of the most admired companies in the United States sat down to make a video the company planned to distribute to all employees. The idea was to convey four values that the leaders said should govern everything that happened in the organization. The four values? Respect, communication, excellence, and integrity. In the video, the CEO was especially emphatic about that last value:

> [We are] a company that deals with everyone with absolute integrity. We play by all the rules; we stand by our word. We mean what we say; we say what we mean. We want people to leave a transaction with [us] thinking that they've been dealt with in the highest possible way as far as integrity and truthfulness, and really doing our business right.

As you might have guessed, the CEO and COO were Ken Lay and Jeff Skilling, and the company was Enron. This example underscores the timelessness of the observation that theologian Reinhold Niebuhr made over 70 years ago when he spoke of the human tendency to express our values "most pretentiously . . . most convincingly . . . at the very moment when the decay which leads to death has already begun."

Now, we're not suggesting that when you communicate one-word values such as *respect* and *excellence* to your team or organization that you're as cynical or duplicitous as Lay and Skilling. However, if your organization is like most, its stated values (and the posters and plaques on which they're emblazoned) are equally worthless.

The problem starts at the source: Pronouncements of "Our values" often emerge from an executive retreat where a facilitator has led the senior team through the narcissistic ritual of identifying the concepts with which they'd like to imagine themselves associated ("commitment," "fun," "teamwork," etc.). In moments of truth and tradeoff, however, these lists do little to help employees who need to distill a set of acceptable options and make a wise selection from among the alternatives. This is why employees hate it when you come down from the mountaintop to share the contents of those self-indulgent lists; it compels them to pretend for a time that you've actually given them something useful and something instructive. You haven't.

If you're serious about equipping employees for moments of truth and tradeoff, we know three things that work:

- Clear boundaries—enforced consistently
- Practical rules of thumb
- Realistic scenarios

Bright Lines and Well-Defined Boundaries— Enforced Consistently

Perhaps we're too hard on Enron. After all, Lay and Skilling really did believe in their four stated values—respect, communication, excellence, and integrity—as long as none of those things ever got in the way of making money hand over fist. Of course, making money and delivering results are important in any organization. If that's not happening, you're not going to stay in business. The real question is:

Are there any caveats or constraints? Like Enron, you can create an environment where the de facto value is "anything goes . . . whatever it takes . . . as long as you are delivering results." Or you can communicate what Nobel laureate Thomas Schelling calls "bright lines" and "well-defined boundaries" so that in their pursuit of results and (individual or organizational) self-interests, your employees clearly understand "the things you can never, ever do." The stuff that's off the table.

To deliver the "out of bounds" message with maximum credibility and impact, you can't delegate the responsibility to the human resources (HR) or compliance departments. The medium *is* the message, which means that employees need to hear it from their leadership.

Nobody does this better than Vanguard, one of the world's largest investment management companies. If you're one of Vanguard's 12,500 employees, you've very clear about what's out of bounds—the stuff you can never do. You learned it in your first week of work, possibly in a face-to-face setting from the CEO himself. Before he stepped down as CEO in 2008, Jack Brennan (who remains the firm's chairman) frequently showed up at "new crew orientation" to deliver a message.

"We make mistakes all the time," he'd tell them. "You can make mistakes at Vanguard. But you can never make an *ethical* mistake, period. You violate our sense of the right thing, and I am personally going to run you over in the parking lot. If that makes you uncomfortable, there is a break coming up, and you should leave then. But you can't say you didn't hear it." And then, with their full attention, he recited a list of boundaries: "Violate client confidentiality, and you're out. Accept a gift from a vendor, and you're out. There is no redemption. You send an offensive e-mail, you don't work here anymore."

"Of course," Jack told us, "the 'run you over' bit is hyperbole. And the HR guys hate that I say it," he admitted. "But I do it for a reason. Because it's effective. People get it. I have people saying 10 years later, 'I remember you told me that you'd run me over in the parking lot if I ever did anything ethically wrong.'"

Some CEOs might want to be remembered for something else, but we got the feeling that Jack is perfectly happy with this kind of legacy. "It's important never to give ground," he said. "And you hate to see somebody's career end because they sent some stupid e-mail. But if we give ground, we create gray areas. There is no gray area."

And therein lies the payoff for employees—and for Vanguard: No gray areas means that employees waste little or no time and energy wondering and second-guessing what's really expected, what's really rewarded, and what's really out of bounds. As Jack explains, "This isn't an easy place to work. But our uncompromising approach on ethical mistakes is part of what makes this an easy place *to come to work*. Because we are never going to put you in a compromising position." Over the past decade, how many other firms in the finance industry offered the same perk? How many wish they had?

Of course, your out-of-bounds list is credible and instructive only if you consistently enforce it, even when the offenders are top performers—even if it's someone you've previously designated a saint. Otherwise, all you have is a "list of stuff you can never do—unless we really don't want to fire you," which is guidance your employees will find very difficult to interpret and apply. When you make exceptions, your out-of-bounds list loses its value as a practical, reliable tool to help employees make decisions.

Lots of leaders get this in theory, but when the need to act arises, they make excuses why they can't or shouldn't. Not Terry Mullen. As president of Lincoln Financial Distributors, a subsidiary of the Lincoln Financial Group, Terry knows that keeping boundaries meaningful requires continuous, vigilant reinforcement. A few years ago, at a national sales conference, one of Terry's top people made an inappropriate, off-color remark at the podium. "So we fired him," Terry recalls. "He was shocked. He thought, 'I'm the top guy. They can't fire me.' But we did." Shortly after that, another top performer was caught cheating on his expenses. "And he was gone," Terry says. "If you just say, 'Don't say inappropriate things' and 'Don't cheat' but don't do anything about it, no one will listen. The trick is, you have to follow through."

Practical Rules of Thumb

A *rule of thumb* is defined as "a principle with broad application that is . . . easily learned and easily applied . . . for making some determination."[3] We've found that they can be much more useful than a laundry list of esoteric concepts to employees who are trying to decide what to do *when they don't know what to do*. Here are three examples:

"At Goldman Sachs, We're Long-Term Greedy."

When politicians and pundits cite *greed* as the cause of the financial meltdown that began in 2008, we wish they'd be more precise. After all, *greedy* is a subjective term, a disparaging descriptor of someone else's pursuit of his or her own self-interest. And self-interest is the basis of capitalism—the "invisible hand" that drives our economic engine—imperfectly, to be sure—but more reliably than, say, the ham-fisted central planners in the kind of system that Marx devised. Although this is currently unfashionable to say, Gordon Gekko, the Michael Douglas character in the movie *Wall Street*, was right when he said, "Greed, for lack of a better word, is good. Greed is right; greed works."

Unless it's *short*-term greed. Short-term greed leads smart individuals to do collectively stupid things. And that's what got us into the current mess. Through their actions and inactions, Wall Street CEOs, politicians, and regulators fostered a system that handsomely rewarded short-term risk taking while putting in jeopardy the long-term health of the economy. Short-term greed isn't good, it isn't right, and it doesn't work for long—because it's not sustainable. And *everybody* pays.

This is why you won't be surprised when we reveal to you our all-time favorite declaration of corporate values. In the 1970s, Gus Levy, then managing partner at Goldman Sachs, was asked what made his firm so special. "At Goldman Sachs," Levy responded, "we're greedy, but we're *long-term* greedy."[4]

And he meant it. Stories that demonstrated the "long-term greedy" ethos in action became part of the firm's folklore. For example, after the stock market crashed in 1987, Goldman Sachs faced a $100 million loss—at the time, 20 percent of the firm's earnings—on an underwriting deal to partially privatize British Petroleum. When some of the underwriters began looking for legal technicalities that would reduce their exposure, Goldman Sachs' managing partner at the time, John Weinburg, pushed back:

"Gentlemen, Goldman Sachs is going to do this [deal]. It is expensive and painful, but we are going to do it. Because . . . those of you who decide not to do it . . . won't be underwriting a goat house. Not even an outhouse." And when the resulting loss chased other large firms out of the privatization business in Europe, Goldman Sachs picked up the slack. Long-term greedy paid off. During that same era, Goldman Sachs left short-term money on the table when it refused to represent any company undertaking a hostile bid for another company. Threatened companies, in turn, took their business to Goldman Sachs.[5] Another win for long-term greedy. As the firm grew and grew, this folklore helped untold numbers of employees navigate sticky situations:

"We should do the right thing even if it hurts in the short term because at Goldman Sachs we're long-term greedy."

Now you might be thinking, in light of recent events: How can Goldman Sachs still lay claim to long-term greedy? Why are you glorifying them? They took government bailout money! We'll return to this topic in Chapter 6.

"Our Values, in Order of Importance."

Nguyen Toan runs the PetroVietnam unit that builds refineries and other technical installations. In recent years, the unit has successfully completed 26 projects, with no failures. Ask Toan the secret of his success, and he'll tell you how he relentlessly communicates with his employees about values. "Our top three priorities," he says, "are safety, quality, and productivity." Of course, building refineries is a dangerous, tricky business, and there is constant tension among these three values. So Toan's list of priorities wouldn't offer much practical guidance to employees facing tough day-to-day choices—except that he has made clear the order of importance.

"We make sure that everyone understands that safety is the most important," he says. And it seems to be working. In the past seven years, Toan's team has logged nearly 10 million person-hours and had only one accident—a broken leg. This is an impressive statistic in any industry, let alone in the refinery-building business.

"Then we have quality," Toan says. "At first, our quality was not very good, and after construction, we'd have a lot of repairs and welding to go back and do. We'd spend a lot of time and money doing repairs afterward, delaying schedules. But we started providing incentives for better quality, and we're seeing higher-quality work emerge. But back to safety: If someone is hurt in the process, the quality doesn't matter."

And the third value? "Once we ensure that safety and quality are achieved, we value productivity," Toan says. "We don't push it too hard, though. Because the faster people work, the less safety and less quality there will be."

If your team or organization has a list of stated values, and in their practical application there are tensions among them, you can take the easy way out: List them on a nice poster with seagulls and a windsurfer in the background, hang it up all over the office, and pretend you've done something meaningful. Or you can do what Toan did: List those values in order of importance, equipping your people with a tool that actually helps them to evaluate tradeoffs from situation to situation and to make more confident decisions about which alternative represents "the right thing to do."

"Play Aggressively without Fouling Out."

Lots of leaders say they want employees to innovate and try new things, but then those same leaders punish any risky behavior that doesn't work out. Thus employees learn quickly that the real message is, "Smile and nod your head, but don't really take any chances." But if you're a leader who really does want employees to take risks, how do you encourage them to do it responsibly?

Carlos Nieva, director of services and operations for Alcatel-Lucent in Spain, has earned a reputation for encouraging and holding his people accountable for responsible risk taking. "I use basketball metaphors because I am a basketball fanatic," he told us. "What I say to my people is: 'I expect that when you are on my team you are going to make some mistakes . . . or, in the language of basketball, commit some fouls. When you commit a foul, you raise your hand—admit the mistake—and keep playing. If you never commit any fouls, never make any mistakes, you're probably not playing aggressively enough or with enough competitiveness or intensity. On the other hand, if you get into foul trouble—if you commit too many mistakes—then you're out of the game. And if you're out of the game, you're not helping the team.'"

He adds: "The other thing is: Sometimes basketball players commit fouls because they are playing aggressively, but other fouls are just obvious mistakes. You don't want to keep a player in the game who commits flagrant fouls. We're going to pull those players off the court." Even if they are not as passionate about basketball as Nieva, his employees find that this metaphor offers practical guidance in moments of truth and tradeoff, helping them appropriately balance the need to innovate with the need to manage risks.

In the Heat of the Moment,
Do People Honor Their Pledges?

According to the *New York Times*,[6] one-fifth of the MBA grads at Harvard in 2009 took a public pledge to "serve the greater good" and "refrain from advancing their 'own narrow ambitions' at the expense of others." Said one pledger, "We want to stand up and recite something out loud with our class." At Columbia, meanwhile, all MBA grads must pledge to "adhere to the principles of truth, integrity, and respect. I will not lie, cheat, steal, or tolerate those who do."

We admire the intent. But will the pledging make a difference in the actual *behavior* of these future captains of industry?

In answering this question, one may or may not be able to draw useful inferences from the following: A recent study[7] looked at the efficacy of "virginity pledges," which the U.S. government spends millions of dollars each year to support as part of an abstinence program focused on teenagers. The results? Five years after taking an abstinence-till-marriage pledge, pledgers were just as likely as their nonpledging counterparts to have had premarital sex and test positive for a sexually transmitted disease. Also, and conveniently, 82 percent of the pledgers denied ever making the pledge.

We can only hope that one of the Ivies will conduct a similar longitudinal study among its MBA oath takers.

Realistic, Scenario-Based Discussions

When U.S. Airways pilot Chesley "Sully" Sullenberger lost both engines shortly after takeoff from La Guardia in January 2009, he stayed cool and made the right call—to ditch the plane in the Hudson River—because he'd trained repeatedly how to respond in many of the sticky situations a pilot might encounter. Even if the stakes aren't quite as high in your organization's line of work, realistic, scenario-based training is a great idea—if you want your people to stay cool and make smart choices in moments of truth and tradeoff.

For many years, we've helped organizations create scenarios based on real-life situations that employees face. And then we help actual leaders (*not* HR or the compliance departments) prepare to hold face-to-face discussions with small groups of employees around these scenarios—and the right thing to do in the situations described.

In some cases, there are actually "right" answers to the questions, and the discussion provides an opportunity to talk about the application of specific compliance-related rules and procedures to actual sticky situations that employees face. Here's an example of one such scenario and the associated discussion questions:

You and a vendor have developed a great working relationship during the course of a $2.5 million project. The contractor invites you to play golf and have lunch afterward, which you accept. On the way home, you realize you never saw a bill for either the golf *or the lunch—which, as best as you can estimate, may have cost as much as $175.*

- *Did you just commit an act of noncompliance?*
- *Why or why not?*
- *What is the right thing to do?*

Scenario-based discussions such as these are a great way to bring the compliance manual to life and take away your employees' excuses about "gray areas." It lets employees know unequivocally that the organization's compliance policies aren't like the admonition on the Q-Tip box to avoid inserting the product into the ear canal—a perfunctory message that for practical reasons people routinely ignore.

What's even more interesting, however, are the scenarios that are less about compliance and more about reputational judgment—where there are typically no right or wrong answers codified somewhere in the compliance department. Our colleague Barry Mike, an expert in developing these scenarios, notes that clients "are often surprised at how much employees appreciate the opportunity to discuss the practical application of company values to what senior leaders may consider to be relatively mundane but realistic challenges." For example:

Your boss e-mails you and asks you to print out a client document and deliver it to the client within the next hour. While printing the document, you notice many typos, spelling, and format errors. Upon reading the document for consistency, you find that it needs a lot of editing. Your boss has told the client that the document will be delivered within the hour, and the client is counting on it getting there on time. However, in order for you to read through the entire document and make the necessary edits, you will need at least two hours. What do you do?

After outlining a scenario such as this one, the leader then facilitates a group discussion around six questions we prescribe:

Which of our values should guide your decisions and actions in this situation?

Are there unwritten rules or precedents in our culture that would suggest how to handle this situation or one like it? If so, are those unwritten rules or precedents consistent with our values?

Would you be likely to seek input from others when deciding how to act? If so, whom would you engage? How would you engage them? What would you say?

Would our values, and the way we apply them, differentiate us in a situation like this? In other words, would you expect us to handle this situation differently than would a competitor?

What positive consequences, if any, would you expect to encounter as a result of making a values-driven decision in this situation?

What negative consequences, if any, would you expect to encounter as a result of making a values-driven decision in this situation? How would you manage them?

The discussions around scenarios such as this one are always enlightening for all parties. Employees walk away with more practical clarity about what to do when they don't know what to do (and enhanced perceptions of the leader's credibility). And, as a result of the opportunity to reinforce expectations, leaders come away with more confidence that employees will make smart decisions when it counts. Additionally, as a result of the opportunity to listen to candid input and discussion about challenges employees encounter, leaders typically come away from these conversations with good ideas about steps they can take to create the conditions of accountability more effectively.

Creating Accountability for Legal and Regulatory Compliance

By Barry Mike

Based on my experience helping organizations reduce reputational risk by creating accountability for legal and regulatory compliance, here are my top five coaching points for leaders:

1. *Senior leadership has to own compliance.* When you make your compliance officer, HR, or training team the voice of compliance, you might as well shout, "We're just going through the motions to cover our behinds." In the organizations that most effectively promote compliance, the CEO is front and center on this topic. When senior leaders visibly own compliance, employees are then—and

only then—willing to consider the possibility that this is a topic of real importance and worthy of more attention and commitment than is minimally necessary for CYA purposes.

2. *Make sure that employees can easily access the policies and procedures they need—when they need them, where they need them.* It's not enough simply to have policies and procedures. If you want employees to comply with the rules, they need easy access to them. Dusty binders sitting in some back-office closet won't do, nor will intranet pages buried 10 clicks down. If finding what they need, when they need it, takes more than an extra step outside of normal work procedures, employees won't do it, especially if they believe that taking the time to chase down a policy or procedure will jeopardize their ability to deliver on your other performance expectations. Even if they're just too lazy to search, you've given them a viable excuse if they need to invoke it. So consider investing in an intuitive user interface or well-thought-out information architecture for your intranet to turn your policies and procedures Web site into a useful and *usable* tool.

3. *Make compliance policies and procedures comprehensible to mere mortals.* Policies and procedures are most often written for technical and legal exactitude by auditors, accountants, and lawyers. The result: policies and procedures that can be read and used only by auditors,

accountants, and lawyers. I know of one consultant, a lawyer with an English degree turned corporate trainer, who is making a comfortable living translating policies and procedures into English so that the employees for whom they are intended actually can understand them. The alternative: Incorporate those who actually have to use policies into the process of developing them to ensure that they can be understood.

4. *Engage the frontline in creating policies that fit real-world needs and nuances.* Under the compliance processes that many companies have in place, if every employee followed every policy and procedure "to the letter," business operations would grind to a halt. It's not simply that policies and procedures are written by auditors, accountants, and lawyers in the language of auditors, accountants, and lawyers. Rather, it's that those producing policies and procedures have not spent any time on the front lines, where business is occurring. As a result, the policies and procedures they produce don't take into account, nor integrate, the rules of thumb that workers use on an everyday basis to get things done. Invariably, some of the behaviors people use to produce on the job wind up being noncompliant. Needlessly.

5. *It's more productive to focus on preparing people for sticky situations than to try to improve their personal constitution and character.* Until you have identified and resolved all the systems-related problems that hinder compliance, it's

pointless to invest in character development as a means of increasing compliance. And, when you get to that point, well, it's still pretty much pointless. When was the last time a one-day workshop and the accompanying desk tchotchke changed your fundamental character or the content of your heart? Yeah, same here. So instead of trying to make your people more virtuous, focus on equipping them with stronger situational judgment so that they know what to do when they don't know what to do and so that you can more reliably count on them to make principled decisions in sticky situations.

CHAPTER 2

INVEST EXCRUCIATING MINUTES TO ENSURE ROLE CLARITY

Without clarity about *who* is responsible for performing specific tasks, it's impossible to have accountability. However, exercising the discipline to get that clarity isn't much fun. "In fact," says our friend, Jose-Luis Bretones-Lopez, "it's often excruciating." He should know. He works for a very well-known global company and a few years ago was responsible for introducing more rigor into the way the company operates in one of its major international markets. He wasn't always welcomed with open arms.

"For starters," he says, "the steps involved in 'planning the work' (which includes getting role clarity) feel boring to most people." But that's only part of the problem, Jose-Luis tells us. "Especially in a culture like ours that expects results—delivered quickly and consistently—the response from managers is: 'Why spend a lot of time *planning* to get stuff done when we could actually be *doing* it?'"

How did he respond to that resistance? "I tried to get people to see that the 'ready, *fire*, aim' approach to managing work is actually a very expensive way to do business. It's costly, in terms of money, time, energy, and morale—*and more so than we realize.*" Why is that? "Well," Jose-Luis says, "we don't know specifically what future problems we're preventing by taking the excruciating minutes now to ensure role clarity. If we knew for certain that investing one extra minute now would save us 15 later, we'd do it every time. If we knew for certain that investing 15 hours of time to clarify roles and objectives and decision rights at the beginning of a project would save us 15 weeks later and the incalculable costs of a demoralized team, we'd do it every time. But we don't know any of those things with certainty. The only thing we know for certain is that we have to deliver specific results, and we have a finite amount of time to complete them."

Legal theorist and judge Richard Posner illuminates this paradox: "One can't expect to receive praise, or even to avoid criticism, for preventing a bad thing from happening unless people are sure the bad thing would have occurred had it not been for the preventive effort."[1] No wonder the cause of disciplined role clarity lacks so few champions!

And yet, as we said at the outset, without clarity about *who* is responsible for performing specified tasks, it's impossible to have accountability. Besides working to enlighten others about the underappreciated risks and costs of failing to establish role clarity, what else can you do? One solution is to try to reduce the "excruciation factor." To that end, we'll highlight in the rest of this chapter a few minimally painful ways to help ensure role clarity and, by extension, accountability.

Emil's Rule: Assume That There's Confusion until There's Proof That There Isn't

Recently, a marketing team working on a high-stakes project came together for two days to prioritize activities and divvy up responsibilities. At the end of the second day, with everyone exhausted, the leader summarized the notes he'd taken about commitments and next steps. "Are we all on the same page?" Everyone nodded. "Did I miss anything?" Everyone shook their heads.

At this point, our consulting colleague, Emil Bohn, the facilitator, very diplomatically noted for the record that he wasn't buying any of it. Emil believes that in the absence of explicit evidence to the contrary, the default assumption should be that a group of people does *not* have shared understanding about who is doing what by when. Why? Part of it is the inherent frailty of human communication: Of course there are going to be misunderstandings to clarify. But he also believes that there is sometimes a darker motive: "We collude with each other by keeping our requests ambiguous," Emil says. "This provides all parties with an escape route—a convenient excuse they can deploy if needed."

So instead of asking, "Are we all on the same page?" or "What am I missing?" and accepting predictable responses, one should conclude a meeting by going around the room and asking each person to say aloud what they are committing to do and by what date.

And what happened in the important team meeting when the tired participants did as Emil suggested? The same thing that happens every time he tries this experiment: Instant incredulity and scoffing at the prospect of such a mind-numbing activity, followed by resignation to it (Emil never backs down!), followed by the humbling discovery that more than half the people in the room had no idea what they had just committed to do by nodding their heads in agreement.

Maybe this is what seventeenth-century French mathematician and physicist Blaise Pascal had in mind when he said, "All human evil comes from this: Man's being unable to sit still in a room." But if you establish a pattern of asking people at the end of a meeting to explicitly state everything to which they've just committed, they'll learn to pay better attention and more rigorously capture their responsibilities—if only to make it possible to get out of the room faster!

Run the West Coast Offense

Legendary football coach Bill Walsh developed what is popularly known as the *West Coast offense* when he was assistant coach for the Cincinnati Bengals in the 1970s. When he moved on to become head coach of the San Francisco 49ers, the West Coast offense helped Walsh lead the team to three Super Bowl wins. And in the years since, at least a handful of other Super Bowl–winning teams, most with coaches mentored by Walsh, have used the West Coast offense as well. So what is it?

In his penetrating look at the game of football, *The Blind Side*,[2] Michael Lewis notes that with his West Coast offense, Walsh ". . . infused the . . . game with two new qualities: dullness and safety . . . it stripped a lot of the risk out of passing. It was more reliable and less explosive, more mechanical and less obviously artistic."

And it won football games.

Lewis notes that Walsh's ". . . offense felt engineered. The virtues it exalted above all others were precision, consistency, and predictability."

And it was excruciating to practice and perform: "By its very nature, the enterprise demanded tedious repetition: for ball and receiver to arrive on a patch of turf the size of a welcome mat at the same moment, their timing had to be precise. . . . At first Walsh had a problem finding the extraordinary amount of time he needed to practice with his quarterbacks and receivers."

Leadership consultant Lisa Marshall doesn't coach football, but she preaches Bill Walsh–like principles to help her clients learn to manage *requests* and *promises* with precision and predictability. If you've spent time in practice with Lisa, you know there are five elements to what she calls a "complete" request:[3]

- Exactly who is making the request? Is it you, or are you passing on someone else's request?
- Who is the request being made of? ("This needs to be done" is not a clear request of anyone.)
- What specific action are you asking to be taken?
- What specifically are your conditions of satisfaction?
- By when?

This covers the "pass." But what about the "reception"? Lisa coaches the people she works with to become very disciplined in their response to requests of them. They must commit to one of five possible routes:

- *Yes.* This is a commitment to deliver on what was requested. Saying "yes" to a request is a promise. Lisa found that when she coaches people to think of their "yeses" as promises, it helps them confront their habit of overcommitting. "I sometimes put them on 'yes' diets," she says, "where for three weeks they can't say yes to anything on the spot; they can only commit to commit. Then they need to go away and think about it."
- *No.* This is a declined request. It is also a promise: "Not now, not ever."
- *I have to check.* This sounds like "I can't even tell you if I can do that; I have to go back and look at my calendar or I have to check with other people; I'll get back to you by such and such a date [which is a promise]."
- *Counteroffer.* "I can't do that; I could do this." Or "I can't do it by that date, but I could do it by this date."

- *Renegotiate.* This, Lisa explains, is when you made the promise, then stuff happens, and you realize you can't deliver. In that case, it's your responsibility to let people know with enough time that they have an alternative. Hoping that something will change and you'll still be able to pull it off and letting time slip away without telling people you are not going to deliver is absolutely unacceptable.

Does it work? The teams that Lisa has coached have racked up some impressive victories. For example, a few years ago a chip manufacturer was embarking on a major change: redesigning the way in which products were developed and transitioning to globally dispersed, around-the-clock development teams while cutting back resources. Lisa's client knew it wasn't going to pull it off without a new level of precision in the way team members managed requests and promises. So the company brought her in to develop team members' passing and receiving skills. The result? Despite the drastic changes, the organization delivered double the number of products to market, grew its volume almost 40 percent and its market share almost 50 percent, while cutting costs nearly in half. Those are Hall of Fame numbers!

Reduce the Drama with a Minimally Excruciating Approach to RACI

Want to put a colony of chimps into disarray? Mess with their role clarity. Confuse their sense of authority. Researchers have developed a way of measuring stress in baboons (believe it or not) and have been measuring the stress levels in males in the African wild. According to F. De Wall, in *Our Inner Ape*, when hierarchy is in flux, when the baboons are unsure about who is in charge and what roles are being filled by whom, stress increases, and they get "jumpy and paranoid."[4]

In contrast, De Wall tells us, when the colony's roles and decision rights are stable, tension is eliminated, "confrontations become rare: Subordinates avoid conflict, and higher-ups have no reason to seek it. Everybody is better off. The group can hang out together, groom each other, play, and relax because no one feels insecure."

It's pretty much the same with human teams (although we may not be terribly anxious to groom our colleagues). For anyone who's ever been a part of an important project where roles, responsibilities, reporting expectations, and decision rights were unclear, you know the kind of melodrama that can produce. People constantly feel personally threatened: Why is *he* doing that? Who gave *him* the authority to make that decision? Why isn't she doing *that*? Does *he* know something I don't know?

And when people feel threatened, their primitive brains kick into gear, and they go into fight, flight, or freeze mode—which effectively denies them access to the executive function of their brain, the part you're paying them to use. But that's not all: *Fight* means lots of unnecessary tension, conflict, or passive aggression. *Flight* means they'll check out—either by becoming emotionally disengaged or leaving the organization. And *freeze* means paralysis so that stuff isn't getting done.

We live to take gratuitous drama out of the system wherever we can. And the conventional way to do this is with a RACI exercise. A RACI chart, for the uninitiated, is a matrix that lists activities or decisions down the *y* axis and a list of roles across the *x* axis. Then you work through the list of decisions and activities and indicate, for each, who is

- *Responsible (R)*. These people are "do-ers" who perform specific activities and tasks.
- *Accountable (A)*. This person or entity has yes/no decision authority and ultimate ownership. (An article of faith among RACI chartists is that there should be only one *A* per activity or decision.)
- *Consulted (C)*. These people should be asked for their point of view *before* a decision is made or action is taken.
- *Informed (I)*. These people should be told about a decision or action *after* the fact.[5]

Even if you've never done a RACI exercise before, you probably can imagine the problem. Put a matrix that has more than three columns and three rows in front of just about any group (even one that includes people who are on the verge of nervous breakdowns as result of role confusion), and they will look for the nearest fire escape. And for good reason: A RACI chart looks intimidating, and completing it is one of the more tedious activities imaginable.

RACI CHART

Functional Roles

Decisions / Functions	Leadership Team	Project Sponsor	Project Director	Project Manager	Work Stream Lead	Operations Specialist	Associate	Coordinator
Identify potential vendors	I	AC	R	R	R	R		
Assess vendors	I	C	RA	R	R	R		
Send RFPs		I	A	C	C	C		R
Evaluate RFPs	I	AC	R	R	R	R		
Write contract			I	AC	C		R	R
Review contract	I	AC	R	R	R	R		
Approve contract	R	RA	C	I	I	I		
Implement contract	I	I	AC	C	R	R		
Communicate contract	I	I	AC	C	C	C	R	
Monitor contract	I	I	A	C	R	R		

EXAMPLE: TEXT RACI

Project Sponsor

His/her mission is to	Provide resources and decisions to drive the initiative to implementation
He/she has yes/no decision accountability for	Any changes to the budget that exceed spending authority or are out of plan
	Any changes to the business case
	Determining the project lead
	Determining what budget requests to take to the executive team
	Additional external or consulting staffing resources for the work streams
He/she is responsible for	Delivering updates to the executive team
	Sending communications at the project team's request
	Advocating for the initiative
	Providing feedback about the system, people, budget, etc.
	Providing resources
	Removing obstacles
	Managing his stakeholders
We should consult him/her before/on	Making technology and design decisions
	Overall questions where we want advice and counsel
We should inform him/her of	Major project milestones
	Spending decisions that are within project authority but are otherwise unusual

And that's too bad. Because every time we finally convince a group to do a RACI exercise, they invariably express the wish that they'd done it sooner.

To make RACI easier to embrace, two of our colleagues, Alan Nelson and Tanya Mann, created a solution: Text RACI. Start by listing the groups or individuals involved in a project, and list them in order of status (high to low). Then, for each group or individual, articulate what they're responsible for, what they're accountable for, when they get consulted, and when they should be informed. See examples on pages 34 and 35.

Why does this more in-depth approach work when a traditional RACI chart doesn't? Two things: (1) It doesn't have the scary visual of the matrix that freaks people out, and (2) it focuses first on the people who leader audiences most like to think about—themselves. And in the process of rationalizing their own decision rights and responsibilities, leaders get more clarity and want to weigh in on the decision rights and responsibilities of the people a level or two below. If the leaders check out of the process after that, it's usually okay; they've weighed in and validated where it is most important for them to do so.

Bodhisattvan Enlightenment

In Buddhism, there are two ways to think about how to achieve nirvana, the end of suffering. One way is to take responsibility for earning enough points to cancel out the karmic deficits you racked up in your previous lives. Once that happens, you're in the clear—removed from the world and all its concerns.

Some Buddhists, however, concluded that the first approach failed to take into account all the interconnections of the system. Yes, each person bears responsibility for his or her own choices. But, given our interdependencies, they said, it makes more sense to approach enlightenment as a collective effort. They conceived of a new ideal, called a *bodhisattva*. A *bodhisattva* is someone who says, essentially, we're *all* going to suffer until we *all* get enlightened.

We work with lots of people who are trying to lead without excuses in complex environments with lots of interdependencies. There are

- *Vertical interdependencies* (To deliver on the expectations to which I've committed, what do I need from the people above me or below me on the organization chart?)
- *Horizontal interdependencies* (What do I need from team members or people in other functions?)
- *Process interdependencies* (What do I need from other players upstream or downstream?)

And many of these people are suffering. The problem with highly interdependent systems is that just one nonperformer can muck up the whole thing, creating excuses for everyone else. Those excuses often begin with the words *until* or *yeah, but.* As in

- "Until information technology (IT) gets its act together and clears up their logjams, I'm not going to worry about this project. I'll start caring when they do."
- "Yeah, I know I said I was going to get this to you by the 18th, but Steve's group is late and hasn't sent over its analysis yet."

What is a bodhisattva to do? Follow the twofold path.

Responsibility Chains

We developed *responsibility chains* as a way to help would-be bodhisattvas take excuses out of the system. It's really simple, but it demands the discipline to bring people together for a detailed discussion. In that discussion, you've got to insist on clarity about who—at each level of the organization, at each step in a process, and/or across each functional silo—is going to do what to solve a problem or achieve a goal.

How much detail is enough? In one respect, this is easy. If you require the participants to sign their name to the completed responsibility chain, thereby waiving their right to make excuses later about not having clear and credible expectations, they'll figure out on their own how much detail they need before they pick up a pen.

Note that you won't end all suffering by creating explicit responsibility chains. There will still be failures of performance. But with the enlightenment that comes from responsibility chaining, you'll endure less finger-pointing and be able to make smarter choices about how to respond to the performance failure—including whether you need to remove some people from the system so that they can reconcile their karmic debts in somebody else's universe.

Here are a couple of examples.

When Bad News Isn't Communicated Upward

A leadership team asked us to help them improve the conditions of accountability within their organization. One of the problems we identified in our assessment process is that employees weren't communicating bad news upward. We advised leadership that merely repeating what they'd already said through formal internal communication channels—that they wanted to hear what was happening even if it was negative—wasn't going to do much good.

Instead, we helped the team assemble advisory teams of employees and middle managers to identify the excuses and make commitments to take them out of the system. Predictably, the employee representatives claimed they didn't really understand the expectation to communicate bad news upward and invoked persuasive anecdotal evidence to explain why they feared leadership would punish the messenger if they actually did what leadership was asking them to do. The middle managers in the room claimed that no one had ever told them what they were supposed to do relative to this topic, which they said explained the entirely inconsistent set of practices among managers when it came to the upward communication of bad news.

Instead of arguing with the other participants' perceptions or debating the legitimacy of their excuses, the leadership team focused the discussion on taking the excuses out of the system—legitimate or not. "What do we all have to do," they asked, "to get to the point where bad news flows upward, no excuses?" As a result of the discussion that followed, leadership committed to communicate its expectations more explicitly and consistently, line up rewards for the behaviors it wanted to see, and sponsor new feedback processes to make it easier and safer to push bad news up.

The representatives of middle management agreed to help design and provide simple training for their peers to help them (1) communicate senior leaders' expectations more effectively, (2) shepherd negative information up the chain of command, and (3) reward people who do the right thing.

And finally, the employee representatives helped to design an advisory group that became a primary, credible, and highly effective means of pushing bad news upward. Additionally, because they were committing on behalf of the other employees they represented, they agreed to act as advocates and coaches with their peers. It worked, almost immediately increasing the frequency with which senior leaders got the "heads up" they needed to address small problems before they became big ones (Figure 2-1).

Figure 2-1 Responsibility Chaining: Example 1

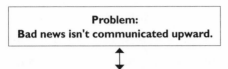

Problem:
Bad news isn't communicated upward.

- Take managers seriously when they say, "We really know what the risks are."
- Participate in sounding board sessions.
- Coach each other, where and how, and where in the chain of command.

- Explain and clarify expectations from senior leadership to employees.
- Put messages into context.
- Reward and recognize those who demonstrate the courage to share "bad news" in a timely fashion.

- Explicitly communicate expectations.
- Reward and recognize those who courageously share "bad news" in a timely fashion.
- Sponsor creation of new systems/processes to make it easier to communicate "bad news" upward.

Who needs to do what at each level to take excuses out of the system?

IT Systems Crash

In another case, a complex organization's system crashes were jeopardizing safety, productivity, and service. In such a situation, it would be tempting for each of the responsible parties, spread across multiple functional silos, to point fingers at each other instead of solving the problem. But they also knew that wasn't acceptable or viable. So they got together, moved beyond the blame shifting, and clarified the commitments everyone needed to make in a highly complex, interdependent system to solve the problem. They also decided when and how they'd get together on a regular basis to review progress and hold each other accountable. It wasn't easy, but it worked, and availability levels soon returned to an acceptable, industry-standard level (Figure 2-2).

Get the Right People in the Room, Be Patient, and Listen

Lisa Bauer is the senior vice president at Royal Caribbean who led its sales organization from worst to first in the industry. How did she do it?

"Among other things, we needed to work together much more effectively with other functional areas, like revenue management, trade support, and marketing," she says. "All of us were working fairly independently. We didn't understand what anybody else was doing. So we had no clear or shared vision of where we were going."

Recognizing this, Lisa and her peers created a Friday morning meeting with the senior leaders from the various areas. "It started out as screaming matches," she recalls. "But over the years it evolved to become the place where everyone provided input and we worked through decisions. That process continues today. The key is having the right people in the room who can make decisions."

Figure 2-2 Responsibility Chaining: Example 2

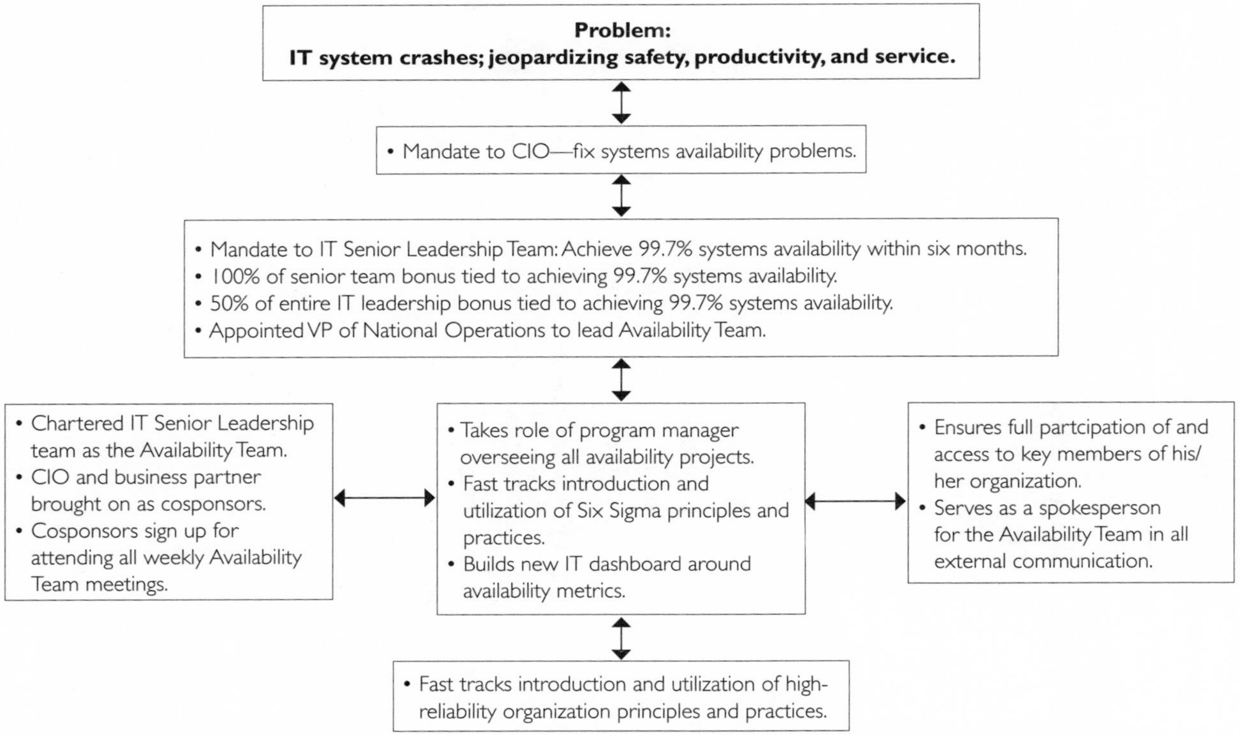

Problem:
IT system crashes; jeopardizing safety, productivity, and service.

- Mandate to CIO—fix systems availability problems.

- Mandate to IT Senior Leadership Team: Achieve 99.7% systems availability within six months.
- 100% of senior team bonus tied to achieving 99.7% systems availability.
- 50% of entire IT leadership bonus tied to achieving 99.7% systems availability.
- Appointed VP of National Operations to lead Availability Team.

- Chartered IT Senior Leadership team as the Availability Team.
- CIO and business partner brought on as cosponsors.
- Cosponsors sign up for attending all weekly Availability Team meetings.

- Takes role of program manager overseeing all availability projects.
- Fast tracks introduction and utilization of Six Sigma principles and practices.
- Builds new IT dashboard around availability metrics.

- Fast tracks introduction and utilization of high-reliability organization principles and practices.

- Ensures full particpation of and access to key members of his/her organization.
- Serves as a spokesperson for the Availability Team in all external communication.

43

But how did they get past the screaming? "Listening," she says. "For the first time, we sat down with Revenue Management and really listened to understand their objectives. And then shared our own. With that approach, we quickly got to the point that we both started to see what was important. That made it possible to make good decisions for everyone, for the company, not just our own department."

Building mutual trust also made it possible for them, as necessary, to agree to disagree. "A lot of times we are at odds about what we want to do," she says. "But no one takes it personally."

She continues: "So when people come in and say, 'What does it take to be successful here?' the first thing I say is develop cross-functional relationships and communication. Really, when we do fall down, it's because somebody wasn't aware that somebody else was doing something."

"As opposed to just focusing on your part," Lisa says, "think 'whole system' "—or, if you prefer, "bodhisattvan."

USE COMMANDER'S INTENT TO PROMOTE OWNERSHIP, STRETCH YOUR PEOPLE, AND ALIGN THEM WITH YOUR BUSINESS STRATEGY

Investing excruciating minutes to ensure clarity about *who* is responsible for doing particular tasks, which we described in Chapter 2, takes time. The good news? The advice we give you in this chapter—for getting clear about the *what* and *how* related to projects, initiatives, and strategy—will save you time while helping you to create the conditions of accountability and deliver results.

Dr. Richard Stotts leads a team at the Air Force Research Laboratory in Dayton, Ohio, where they develop tools and technology for countering weapons of biological and chemical warfare. The stakes are high, and so are his expectations of his team. Richard says that his day-to-day management style reflects an important lesson he learned over 40 years ago at Officer Candidate School (OCS) at Fort Knox.

One day his OCS class was marched double-time to a site where they found a small group of soldiers—a staff sergeant, two corporals, and four privates—as well as a flag pole, shovels, posthole diggers, a wheelbarrow, and several bags of cement mix. The tactical training officer divided the class into several small groups and told them to create a plan to erect the flagpole. Richard felt very fortunate to have a mechanical engineer and a civil engineer in his group. "Because of our combined education and experience, we felt very confident that our team would come up with the best solution," he recalls. "Something that would propel us to the top of our class or at least save us from dozens of push-ups or yards of painful low crawling."

They set to work. The mechanical engineer estimated the wind stress on the flagpole with the flag attached so that they would know how deep to dig the posthole. Then the civil engineer used that data to determine the diameter of the hole based on the volume of cement available, carefully subtracting the volume of the inserted flagpole. And Richard's unique contribution? Having worked on power-line crews before joining the military, he possessed secret knowledge: the ability to use a plumb bob to accurately align the pole in the exact vertical position.

As each group was called up to give its presentation, describing in detail the various plans and associated task assignments, Richard's team maneuvered to go last, not wanting to reveal its superior calculations or the plumb-bob secret.

Finally, with great self-assurance, Richard came forward to present. He described his team's solution, invoking the exacting specifics provided by the engineers before offering a short primer on plumb-bob use. On the faces of the other teams he saw resignation and acknowledgment as they visibly began to accept defeat.

The tactical training officer then called the men to attention and told them that no one had the correct solution and ordered them, on account of their stupidity, to assume the push-up position. While they completed push-ups, he explained that the correct solution would have been to say: "Sergeant, put up the flagpole, and report to me when you are finished. I will be in the mess hall drinking coffee if you have any questions."

"I've found over the years that using this principle—communicating a clear goal and then giving a team autonomy in how to accomplish it—encourages initiative, instills confidence, and develops leadership in subordinates," Richard says. "I also discovered that once the sergeant installed the flagpole, he would see to it that the paint never peeled nor rusted as long as he was present. He had in fact assumed ownership of the flagpole. I no longer had to worry about maintaining the flagpole. But when I ignored the principle of responsible delegation, giving out detailed instructions, and carefully supervised a project, I became the owner and had to maintain it throughout its existence."

Of course, there will be times—metaphorically speaking—when the flagpole will lean a little or be installed upside-down. "So it's a good idea," Richard says, "to glance out of the mess hall window occasionally to see how the task is progressing. If you observe a problem, casually walk by the sergeant as you go to motor pool, find an excuse to take him aside, and suggest a course correction in private. That way the flagpole is still straight, he maintains the respect of his team, and you do not have to assume responsibility for the flagpole for the rest of its existence."

A couple of decades after Richard learned this leadership lesson at Fort Knox, the Army formalized the concept of *commander's intent* (CI). As brothers Chip and Dan Heath described it in their bestseller, *Made to Stick*, "CI is a crisp, plain-talk statement that appears at the top of every order, specifying ... the end-state of an operation. ... When people know the desired destination, they're free to improvise, as needed, in arriving there."[1] In the rest of this chapter we'll look at the uses and advantages of communicating expectations via CI.

Promoting Ownership

As the parable of the flagpole suggests, one of the great advantages of communicating project expectations via CI is that it promotes a sense of ownership. This is especially true for knowledge workers, who, as expert Thomas Davenport knows, thrive on autonomy. "One important aspect of knowledge workers," Davenport says, "is that they don't like to be told what to do . . . almost all knowledge workers need to feel that they have participated in the design or redesign of their work."[2]

Jim Crawford, regional chief information officer (CIO) at a well-known health care organization, stumbled on this insight when he was working in France as a young information technology (IT) manager. He didn't know how to speak French, and he found himself leading a meeting one day where he wanted to provide all the answers but, with a limited understanding of the language, could only pose the problem and ask the group to discuss possible solutions.

"I knew where I would have gone with the answer in the first five minutes," he says. "I mean, I was young and thought I *always* knew the answers. And 55 minutes later, they came up with an answer—the same one I'd been thinking all along."

But he realized that the language barrier that required him to stay silent ultimately saved him time. "They got to do it their way. And I didn't have to go back and convince them of anything, because they came up with the idea," he says. "They owned it. I had complete buy-in to a great solution without even trying. Ever since then, I've been very careful not to provide the solutions. I just lead people and let them get to the answer themselves. And they come up with a great solution that they're all already behind."

Of course, and as Dr. Stotts acknowledged, sometimes it's not enough to communicate your CI and then just lounge in the mess hall—or the equivalent. The leader's job after communicating a desired end state is to keep people focused on the goal and to coach them toward it.

Bob Groody, chief operations officer (COO) of GMAC Bank, believes that starting with the end in mind is essential to keeping a complex project on track. But people get sidetracked and need to be reminded: "This is what I want this thing to look like in the end."

"You may find yourself repeating the same sentences over and over again," Bob says, "but that's often what it takes to keep the focus on your intended result."

Bob likes to give people space to come up with their own ideas. "We get into a room and just throw Post-its® up on the board with different ideas," he says. "Then I have everyone take a step backward and take it in for a few minutes without talking about it. The top three or four ideas usually arise organically, and we'll start working on those. Things can really blossom from this simple process."

In these sessions, Bob always positions himself as coach/facilitator. "Because of my position, people wait for me to talk first. But I avoid it. I don't want the only voice people hear in the meeting to be mine. We get a better result if everyone has a voice." And if the project involves multiple concept meetings, he'll attend just the first few. "Not because I don't have time," he says, "but because I don't want to steer the group in a direction that I'm biased toward. I can play a part in the initial design, but I want to rely on other people to develop and deliver it."

McDonald's CIO Dave Weick sums it up: "A huge part of what accountability means is providing people with enough freedom to solve problems. My job is to ensure they have clarity about what success looks like and then to provide coaching, tools, and resources; give them credit where it's earned; and, as needed, deflect heat."

Stretching Your People

Another advantage of communicating strategic expectations via CI is that you can develop your people—particularly your high potentials and your save-ables—while getting things done. When it works, it's good for everybody. You and the organization win because you've optimized a human resource and nurtured an up-and-comer. The employee wins because figuring out how to deliver successfully on your CI is in many respects its own reward.

We're going to get a bit ahead of ourselves—compelling consequences is the next section of this book—but what we need to call out here is how important it is to know the difference between a "cool challenge" and torture. When is communicating aggressive expectations via CI a reward? When is it punishment? Let's look at an example.

Gordon Xu had a huge challenge. He runs operations in China for chemical-maker FMC's Agricultural Products Group. "When we originally built our plant in Suzhou," he says, "it was on the outskirts of the city. But, like lots of cities in China, Suzhou grew dramatically, and as it expanded, we found ourselves in the middle of new urban development. The government instructed us to relocate. So I called Milton." Milton Steele leads the Agricultural Products Group from FMC's headquarters in Philadelphia. "He said, 'There's no budget for this. Use all local resources; we're not sending any. And I expect you to do this with a perfect safety and environmental record. I know for sure that you can do it. But if you really need help, call me, anytime.'"

Is this a good use of CI or merely a ridiculous assignment? Actually, in this case, we'd say Milton made *great* use of CI—because his charge met all four of the following criteria:

1. Gordon knew exactly the conditions under which he could declare victory: Moving the factory—with local resources and no additional budget.
2. Gordon knew the constraints under which he was operating: He had free reign as long as the accidents or environmental issues (and no budget used).
3. Milton offered *just enough* support: "If yo my help, call me, anytime."
4. The assignment stretched Gordon's cap capacities without exceeding them. For 99 people of 100, what Milton asked Gordon to do might have represented negligence. Ultimately, the difference in this case between a bad expectation and a great expectation was whether Milton knew Gordon well enough to calibrate Gordon's capability.

So how did it work out? "We did it," Gordon says, "with a little technical support that we requested from Philadelphia, a perfect safety and environmental record, and with money from the sale of the old plant. The use of local resources, know-how, and *guānxi*[3] reduced the time needed to execute this project by months. If another multinational chemical company had done this, they'd probably have sent a dozen experts to China for six months!" Gordon is proud of the outcome of the project, was excited to take on the responsibility, and was motivated that FMC's leadership had total confidence in him to deliver. "I also knew that if I ran into some really big problems," he says, "I was not alone. In FMC we believe that a cry for help is not seen as a sign of weakness but as a sign of strength."

Milton modestly downplays the suggestion that this story reflects his possession of some unique leadership insight. "We have to run lean. We're trying to be very clear when we bring people on board that this is a very demanding place to work. There's not much handholding. But we can offer the kind of career-development experiences that make our people, as we say, 'ready for anything.'"

As we emphasized earlier, it's important in formulating your CI to calibrate capabilities accurately. And sometimes that's difficult to know. In such a case, you may need to engage people to test the limits of what's possible and overcome their resistance.

Randy Gier is executive vice president of marketing and research and development (R&D) for the Dr. Pepper/Snapple Group, where they are working continuously to push the company ahead with new ways of meeting consumer needs. "And that generally means that the technology or the ability to get there hasn't yet been explored," Randy says. "I'm talking about the real breakthrough stuff that hasn't been done before and that's going to double your growth."

So he's constantly up against the question: Can it be done? And the people who are challenging him—telling him "We don't know how to get there"—are experts: PhDs in molecular biochemistry, operations management, and process engineering.

Randy's solution is to meet them one on one. "Look," he'll say, "I really want to understand where you're coming from because I'm not a molecular biochemist, so I want to understand a little bit about molecular biochemistry." Then he asks questions. "Okay, well, now I get *that*, but what about *this*? Does it make sense if we thought about it this way?" Often, the answer is, "No, no, Randy, that doesn't make any sense at all." And so he keeps at it, asking questions to understand and exploring other possibilities. "Because I'm respecting their expertise," he says, "but helping them to understand the problem I'm trying to solve, they almost inevitably take me up on the challenge and find a way to apply their expertise to solve the problem." Accordingly, by the time he solidifies his CI, there's already shared agreement (and enthusiasm) around what's possible.

Before we move on, let's note one other thing about using CI to stretch your people. Not everyone is looking for the challenging new opportunities. Take this into account *if they're otherwise providing tremendous value in their current role.* Most people want to be challenged—but not all. CIO Jim Crawford says that he actively looks to identify among his people the high performers who are already working at their preferred potential. "They're of the mind-set, 'I just want to perform really high at the level I am right now. I'm fine with that.' That's a high performer who will stay a high performer. Don't punish them for wanting to stay at a level they enjoy. Just make sure they're doing it well."

The Clearly Undefined Expectation

This "stretching" technique is a derivative of CI, as Carlos Nieva, director of services and operations for Alcatel-Lucent in Spain, explains:

I'm obsessed with the idea that people can deliver in many cases much more than what we as leaders, as managers, as organizations give them the opportunity to accomplish. When we draw an organizational chart, when we set up objectives, when we go through the whole formal process, people tend to think, "Well, this is what is expected out of me and so this is what I want to deliver." In other words, "Tell me how you will measure me, and I will tell you how I will behave." And from that standpoint, I'm obsessed about making sure those expectations are clear.

On the other hand, I don't want those expectations to limit what anybody can bring to the game once they know what the game is about . . . who we're competing against . . . what it takes to win. So I say: "Those are the formal expectations of the role. Now what else are you going to bring to the organization that, unless *you* bring it, we're not going to get?" And when we are looking at performance for the last six months or the last year, I challenge my people: "You did many good things, things that any good professional would have accomplished. What's the difference that *you* made?"

So we have the very clearly defined expectations. And then the clearly *un*defined expectation.

As an example, I just talked to one of our operations guys. New business development is nowhere in his job description. But because of his engagement with a customer, he saw an opportunity, didn't feel limited by his role, and brought the business home.

Aligning Your People with Your Business Strategy

Another advantage of communicating expectations via CI, the Heath brothers explain, is the ability to "align the behavior of soldiers at all levels without requiring play-by-play instructions from their leaders."[4]

An effective expression of CI can get everyone focused on and talking about their role in producing strategic outcomes—instead of just tactical activities. "I don't care how many meetings you attend, how many e-mails you answer, how many committees you're on," says ADT executive Georgia Eddleman. "I care about what you're doing to get us closer to the targeted end state, whether that's improved quality, increased profit margins, reduced costs, or something else. That's what we're going to talk about, report, evaluate, and compensate. We'll connect it to every single level of the organization in a tangible way, every day."

That's not all. An effective expression of CI equips employees at all levels with a single criterion against which to evaluate what otherwise might be tough decisions. Herb Kelleher, Southwest Airlines' legendary CEO, understood this well, as reflected in a story he related to James Carville and Paul Begala:[5]

"I can teach you the secret to running this airline in thirty seconds. This is it: Southwest is the low-fare airline. Not a low-fare airline. We are THE low-fare airline. Once you understand that fact, you can make any decision about this company's future as well as I can."

"Here's an example," Herb said. "Tracy from marketing comes into your office. She says her surveys indicate that the passengers might enjoy a light entrée on the Houston to Las Vegas flight. All we offer is peanuts, and she thinks a nice chicken Caesar salad would be popular. What do you say?"

Paul stammered. So Herb told him: "You say, 'Tracy, will adding that chicken Caesar salad make us THE low-fare airline from Houston to Las Vegas? Because if it doesn't help us become the unchallenged low-fare airline, we're not serving any damn chicken salad.'"

How do you know if your expression of CI will be effective at promoting strategic alignment down and across your organization? It must be

- Simple enough that everyone can understand it.
- Broad enough that anyone at any level of your organization can translate it into action.
- Aligned with everything that *you* are doing. In other words, you can explain how any decision you make or

action you take supports the end state described in your expression of CI.

One of the mistakes that lots of leaders make is they communicate a new business strategy to employees without first translating it into an effective expression of CI. For example, a large multinational company recently invested significant resources to communicate to its employees the following strategy:

We will . . .

- Focus investment spending

- Promote a cost-saving culture

- Routinely review our portfolio, making certain that retaining a business is better for our stockholders than divesting it

- Grow our international business

- Tie management compensation to the company's financial performance

This might be sound business strategy but it's a lousy expression of CI. Why? It's neither simple nor broadly actionable. The vast majority of the organization plays no direct or indirect role in "focusing investment spending," "routinely reviewing our portfolio," or "tying management compensation to performance." And few employees get excited about a strategy they can't do anything to support. The one element of this strategy that everyone in the organization *can* act on is "promote a cost-savings culture." However, if all you really want is for them to find new ways to cut costs, don't hide it or obfuscate it, just say it!

What's the alternative? If a client asked us to help them retool a message like this one so that it fulfills the three criteria for an effective expression of CI, we'd focus on a theme such as "making smarter choices about how we invest our resources." Everyone in the organization has resources—time and energy, if not human capital and budget—and so everyone can translate it into action. And senior leaders then could position their efforts to focus investment savings, review the portfolio, and revise the compensation system as examples of what they are already doing to act on the strategy (which provides evidence that the strategy is "real" and therefore worthy of being taken seriously).

Framing Commander's Intent

Here's a story about a leader who started off on the wrong foot—then got back on track and created widespread strategic alignment by effectively communicating his business strategy as CI:

Max had just come on board as CIO and was traveling around the country to speak to IT employees in each region. On his first stop in Chicago, he stood before 450 IT employees in a large hotel conference room. Everyone was asking themselves the same two questions: Who is this guy? And will there continue to be a role for me in his organization?

Max did a great job, talking about his background, values, and experience. After 20 minutes, he took questions. One employee stood up and asked, "What would you say is your most important priority?" Max said, "I'm going to be spending the majority of my time and energy over the next few months working on a new governance model."

Then someone else asked, "What can we do to help you with your top priority?"

"In the near term," Max answered, "we're putting together some cross-functional advisory teams, and we're going to need two people from Chicago."

That comment, unfortunately, provoked anxiety. Why? At the beginning of the meet and greet, Max had 450 people walk into the room wondering whether they should be polishing their résumés. And by the end, 450 people walked out with orange squishy tchotchkes that said "Governance," thinking, "Two of us will get a chance to support the new CIO's agenda. But 448 of us are screwed."

But why blame Max? He told the truth! In the near term, he needed only a fraction of the workforce to directly support him in implementing his top priority. The problem is that he talked about what action he was planning to take without also communicating an expression of CI with which everyone else could align.

To his credit, he figured out the problem, and before the next stop on his tour, Max got clear about what he needed to communicate. "To support the mission of the organization, we have to get everyone in IT focused on three things: improving the services we deliver, enhancing our organizational and individual capabilities and effectiveness, and reducing costs."

He talked about his immediate focus on governance and how it supported each of the three parts of his message. He then challenged everyone in the organization to align his or her own energies and priorities with it. And he held them accountable for finding "one new thing" they could do immediately, beyond their existing efforts, to help translate his CI into action. Beyond that, he aligned measurement and reward systems with the message and cascaded it through the organization so that everyone at every level was working from a plan that aligned all the way up to Max's.

Within just a few months, employee surveys showed that more than four-fifths of employees in Chicago—and across the country—understood Max's message, believed it was credible, and could articulate what they were doing to directly support it.

CHAPTER 4

COMPETE FOR ATTENTION

A ll the other advice we offer about creating and communicating clear and credible expectations presumes that your people are actually paying attention to what you're communicating. But truth be told, that's something not to take for granted, especially in larger, complex organizations.

Suppose that you need your employees to line up behind you in support of some new program, initiative, or strategy. And they just don't seem to be getting it—even though you've communicated repeatedly. Are they stupid?

Maybe not. The problem might be *rational ignorance*. This is what economists call it when consumers determine that the value of becoming informed about something isn't worth the time and energy costs involved. From this perspective, paying attention is an irrational activity.

Rational ignorance explains all kinds of behaviors. For example, in many organizations, employees may anticipate that investing the time, attention, and energy to isolate, focus on, and process your messages—in a workplace increasingly crowded with noisy information overload—isn't worth the investment. Many employees may interpret your new initiatives as just another management "flavor of the month" or, even worse, consultant speak.

In this chapter we'll suggest three ways to compete more effectively for your employees' attention—so that they're more likely to invest the time and energy to understand and deliver on your expectations.

Rationalize Supply against Demand

As the influential social scientist Herbert Simon observed four decades ago, attention is a scarce resource (even if we don't tend to think of it that way), and therefore, "a wealth of information creates a poverty of attention."[1] There's only so much of it to go around. Which is why you can't expect employees to pick out and pay attention to your genuinely important messages if you've flooded the market with cheap imitations.

Supply-side communication is a misguided activity that often flows from good intentions: "We just did something. And communication is good. *Ergo*, let's communicate what we just did." In other cases, leaders make supply-side communication choices because it makes them feel good—for example, to show off all the important stuff they're doing—or just because they can (e.g., "We have a cool studio, so let's make some videos.").

In any case, supply-side communication choices—instead of producing the utopian ideal of the "fully informed employee"—create an environment where everyone just ignores most of the information delivered through formal channels while wondering what the hell is really happening—and what things they really ought to get on board with.

One CEO who understands, perhaps better than most, the importance of demand-driven communication is Gen-Pacific's Thanh Trinh. When he was a kid growing up outside Hanoi, most of the books in the local bookstore came from Moscow. To encourage reading, state-run publishers sent lots and lots of books and priced them very inexpensively. Thanh and his friends made frequent visits to the bookstore. "But not," he confesses, "because we were voracious readers." They found that they could buy stacks of subsidized books, remove the covers, and take them to the recycling center and turn a profit. "So the books were very valuable to us," Thanh recalls, "but not in the way intended."

The insights from that experience influence the way Thanh communicates with his employees today. "I run the company, so they always listen respectfully when I'm talking," he says. "But I always ask myself: 'Am I really giving them valuable information?'"

He's learned that what his employees appreciate most are conversations that address three questions: (1) "Who are we, and how do we make money?" (2) "How are we different from the competition, or how are we *trying* to be different from the competition?" and (3) "What do our customers really need, and how can we work together more effectively to address those needs?" By focusing his leadership communication on the actual information demands in the system, Thanh has the attention he needs from employees when he communicates his expectations.

The same is true of Chris Franklin. He's a regional president at Aqua America, a water utility company that serves 3 million people in 13 states from Maine to Texas. "I've watched a lot of utility managers walk into the garages and say, 'I need more productivity,' and throw a bunch of swear words around, which is kind of fun and all," Chris told us, "but that's not what the employees there are looking for."

What they're looking for, he says, is the same kind of respectful communication that you would get in a management briefing. "Yes, you need to tailor your message to the audience," Chris says. "But those employees want to know how the company is performing on Wall Street, why the stock is down, what's happening with earnings, how they fit in, and how we are going to control operating expenses to make our budget." They want to know those things, he believes, because they want to contribute. "And," he adds, "because they want to be smart about the company, like everyone else. When they are asked a question by a customer, friend, or family member, if they are 'in the know' about the company, they are a better ambassador for the company than anybody else in the organization." But most important, by addressing their information needs, Chris has the attention of his employees when he needs it to get them aligned with his expectations.

Go Organic

To make fun of the overhyped messaging that so many organizations and consultants create, we invented the term *P-NAFBI*™, which is short for *Proper Noun and Acronym-Free Business Initiative*—a concept for which we sometimes seem to be the only advocates. Hopefully, we're not just entertaining ourselves with our tongue-in-cheek mockery. We're trying to make a point, which is this: In many organizations, the amount of attention that employees will pay to any new thing that leaders introduce is inversely proportional to the amount of branding, new acronyms and jargon, esoteric and aspirational language (e.g., use of the verb *strive*, which practically no one uses in day-to-day conversation), splash, and gloss associated with its rollout. In reality, low-hype, high-substance communication using organic language works best.

One way to meet the demand for organic communication products is to harvest words and themes from real honest-to-goodness, nonartificial, nonsweetened organizational discourse. This is how Vanguard's new, improved mission statement came about, as former CEO Jack Brennan explained to us. "We used to have one of those multiple-bullet-point mission statements," he says. Then one morning he went to a crew member breakfast where he talked with a small group of employees about "helping clients achieve their financial goals by being the highest-value provider." One of the participants asked: "Isn't this why we are here? That sounds like a mission statement." Jack asked the others, "What do you guys think?" and they said, "Yeah, that is what we are here to do, to help people reach their goals."

So Jack said, "You know what? I have a board meeting tomorrow morning, and I think we are going to change our mission statement." And they did. A few days later, Jack presented the new message at the annual meeting for new crew and asked: "Is this better?" A round of applause told him the answer.

Here Today, Here Tomorrow

It's irrational for employees to pay attention to—and invest effort to align with—any new effort or initiative they believe is "flavor of the month" and will soon be forgotten. And, unfortunately, in many organizations this is the default assumption that most employees hold any time leaders introduce something new. "I've learned from experience," they'll sometimes say, "that *this too shall pass*." You can complain that this is a cynical point of view for them to hold—but most of them arrived at it honestly.

So how do you show your employees that *this time it's for real*?

It starts with the words you use and the consistency with which you use them. "The main thing is to keep the main thing the main thing," as the saying goes. This means that all leaders have to use the same message—and stay on message—over time. When Dr. Len Schlesinger, president of Babson College, was a C-level executive at Limited Brands, he learned both how important and how hard this is to do. He was trained as an academic, so he likes to play with words.

"Every time I used to talk about issues of strategy and positioning and stuff like that, I just used a little bit different phrasing," he says. "Because then it was more interesting to me. And I suddenly discovered that every time I used a little bit different phrasing, all of a sudden, people start saying, 'Oh my God, the strategy's changed again.'"

"I spent about a year screwing up the business by using a few different words every six to eight weeks," Len says. "Then I realized I better just shut up. I better use the same words all the way through." The lesson? "You've got to recognize [that] it's not about just entertaining yourself—unfortunately!"

Len's experience is common. In fact, through our internal tracking studies in dozens of organizations, we discovered a few years ago a phenomenon we call the *puke point*. It refers to the point in time that leaders become so sick of staying on message (and hearing themselves repeat it) that they "want to puke." What's remarkable is that the puke point frequently coincides with an upswing in employee understanding of and engagement around the strategy. In other words, it's important for leaders to stay on message even after they're sick of doing so because that's the critical point in time that employees are just starting to truly "get it." Two other points:

- Keeping "the main thing the main thing" also requires that you explicitly connect the dots for your people, making clear how all your decisions and actions— including what you're measuring and rewarding— support whatever it is you want them to pay attention to and align with. Absent that, you've tipped your hand that whatever you're talking about is likely something in which your interest is ephemeral.
- In short, you've got to visibly practice what you preach. We described earlier how Jack Brennan simplified Vanguard's mission statement; what's even more important is that he lives it. When we went to his office one day to interview him, he was reviewing his travel schedule. He planned to go to Phoenix for the day and then return to Philadelphia for a client meeting. Then he planned to immediately turn around and head back to the West Coast for meetings in San Diego, San Francisco, Los Angeles, and Pasadena. And though he didn't point this out to us, we happen to know that he flies coach. So wouldn't it make a lot more sense, we wondered, to move the Philadelphia meeting instead of making two cross-country trips in a very short period of time? Not

a chance. "The day I say something and don't act on it, I'm no longer credible," Jack told us. "The travel is a real pain. But it's the day that worked best for the Philadelphia client. If I am saying they matter but I won't travel hard to do what works for them, then I am not credible."

Like all great leaders, Brennan understands that he is constantly broadcasting messages to the troops through day-to-day decisions and actions, the things he rewards, what he tells people formally, and what he says informally. By sending steady signals on all frequencies, he can count on Vanguard's thousands of employees to tune in to all his messages.

Along these lines, there are a couple of other actions leaders take that are especially effective for capturing attention and demonstrating the enduring nature of your commitment to something new. One of them is to *stop doing other things*. Lots of times employees won't take a new edict seriously when their reality is that "there used to be eight things that are really super important for everybody to get on board with, and now there are nine." Removing some of those items from the "importance pool" to free up energy, attention, and resources signals that you're serious. Here's an example:

Bob Walton recently took the helm of Qualcomm Enterprise Services, a division of Qualcomm with a proud

18-year history of delivering solutions to the transportation and logistics industry. But they're not as profitable as they were eight years ago. "So I signed up to help develop the business and to make this division more strategically and financially relevant to Qualcomm as a whole," Bob says.

In his first six weeks, Bob spent a lot of time with his people explaining his expectations and where he planned to lead the organization. He also told them that he wanted to create an environment in which it was okay to say "No." As Bob says, "We are here to say no to a bunch of things and yes to a few things, and we're really going to knock the ball out of the park on those few things."

It's one thing to say this in a PowerPoint presentation as part of the standard "Hey, I'm the new guy in charge" road show. But Bob moved quickly to actually halt development on a couple of product lines that people thought were sacrosanct. And, he says, "we began pulling out of a couple of countries where continued focus doesn't make sense given our new strategy." This showed that Bob was serious. What's more, it sent the message to the rest of the organization that it was safe for them to take responsibility for saying "No" in order to throw all the system's energy and talent behind the new strategy.

Another thing that shows that you're serious is *giving the boot* to the people for whom you have created the conditions of accountability but who have chosen not to get on board—your sinners. "I'm happy to help these people leave the organization in a dignified way," says MedeFinance

CIO Dave Watson. "But I can't let them stay, popping up from time to time to blow up train tracks and power poles," he says metaphorically. "As a leader, you absolutely have to hunt these people down and either enroll them in the change you're driving or get them out—because they're toxic. Keeping them around tells the rest of the organization that you're not really serious about making the big change you're espousing. If you don't act, it is tacit permission for everyone to stay where they are."

The coolest thing about effectively competing for attention, staying on message, and showing that you're really serious is that your people are capable of bringing to bear enormous innovation and adaptation once they realize the inevitability of doing so. Randy Geier, currently an executive with Dr. Pepper/Snapple, shares the following experience from his time at Frito-Lay: At a management meeting of the top 150 managers in the business, Randy and his colleagues set a goal of moving their market share from 40 to 60 percent. The managers flipped. "No way," they said.

For two weeks that's all Randy heard people talking about. "This is a ridiculous goal. What is the president smoking? You know how many trucks that would take? Do you know how many plants we'd have to build? Do you know how many potatoes we'd have to buy?"

"All we heard," Randy says, "is 'Can't, can't, can't, can't!'"

But the CEO didn't budge. And once people realized that no one cared about their "What if" and "How many" and "We can't," they started changing their mind-set. They started saying, "Oh, okay. Well, let me tell you how many trucks we're going to need to buy. Let me tell you how many plants we're going to need to build. Let me tell you how many potatoes we're going to have to buy." And people started finding solutions, Randy says. And today, Frito Lay has over 60 percent share.

CHAPTER 5

BOOST THE CREDIBILITY OF YOUR HIGH EXPECTATIONS

In his classic book, *Influence*, Robert Cialdini explains, "As a rule, we most prefer to say yes to the requests of someone we know and like."[1] He goes on to add, "We are more favorable to [those] we have had contact with." That's why we tell our clients that leadership *visibility* and *accessibility* are so important. Employees perceive expectations for high performance to be more credible when they come from a leader they perceive to be "real" and "likeable." (As Marshall McLuhan famously put it, "The medium is the message.")

For the most part, there's no rocket science involved in translating this insight into action. But it does require deliberate attention and action.

Dr. Ken Melani, chief executive officer (CEO) of Highmark, a major health insurer in the Northeast, told us about an elevator ride he took a few years ago that reminded him that simple actions (or inactions) can have tremendous consequences. After a silent ride with several employees up several floors, a colleague told him, "You lost a great opportunity there." Ken asked what he meant, and the colleague said, "Remember when you weren't the CEO and when you rode on the elevator with the CEO? How did you feel when he didn't acknowledge your presence? How did you feel when he said a simple 'Hello'?" Ken appreciated the feedback because he understands what's at stake.

And, truth be told, we think he's an exemplar when it comes to promoting openness and leadership accessibility. We believe that it's a big part of the reason Highmark has been able to build a culture where accountability and performance are high. A recent benchmark study showed that Highmark offers neither the highest salaries nor the richest benefit package relative to its peers. But the company has no problem with recruitment or retention. Why? The openness, Ken says, "ties us together as a group, and that's ultimately what makes people want to come here and stay here."

Tokyo Electron's Vickie Lee has her own simple way of breaking down barriers and establishing connections with employees. "We set up a table out of the main stream of traffic where we all sit around and have lunch every day," she says. "It's gone a long way toward helping people see me as a real person instead of just a title."

At Lincoln Financial Distributors, President Terry Mullen is dedicated to accessibility and to making the company feel like a small, close-knit organization, even though it's growing rapidly. His style is informal. He walks around, regularly visits his employees' offices, and conducts frequent short one-on-one meetings. Terry doesn't allow long periods of time to pass without contact with his direct reports. Rather than waiting for lots of issues to pile up and then going through them in marathon sessions, he'd rather hear about a problem immediately and walk down the hall to deal with it then and there. It's important to him that his people know he's accessible. As he told us, "When they do call, they're always so surprised when I answer my phone, and I say, 'Why wouldn't I pick up? It was ringing.'"

Everybody on the leadership team answers calls on our 800 numbers. Why is that? Well, there are two reasons. One, what are we here to do? We are here to serve clients. It is an intimidating job, those 800 number calls. You don't know: It could be Bill Gates calling or somebody who wants to know whether you'll take a hundred dollars (which we don't). So everybody on the leadership team serves on the 800 numbers because we need to always be in touch with the clients. We can never lose sight of the clients on whose behalf we're working.

The second reason is to send a message. As a Vanguard leader you show up to take calls, and you might be sitting next to a brand-new associate. If you're that new associate, we want *you* to know that *we* know you have the most important job in the company. I can do what I do for a living on Saturday or Sunday or that night. But at 10:22 on a Tuesday morning, the phone is ringing. And whether the new associate takes the call or I take the call, the most important thing we can do is serve the client.

—Jack Brennan, chairman
and former CEO, Vanguard

Sometimes, being visible and accessible and engaging in dialogue are *most* important for boosting the credibility of your expectations when getting out to your people and making yourself a little bit vulnerable may seem like the *last* thing you want to do. Our favorite story for illustrating this concept is about Chris Franklin, regional president of the water utility Aqua America. When Chris joined the company, the variance in productivity among meter readers immediately caught his attention. Some were doing five times as many jobs as others.

So he set out to create credible conditions of accountability, first by clearly communicating his expectations. He brought everyone together and said, "What's in the past is in the past. All is forgiven. But moving forward, let me be very clear about what I expect in terms of productivity. And I think when you look around the room you know who's carrying their weight and who isn't. So, if you hold yourselves accountable and we fix this going forward, we won't have to revisit this conversation."

A month went by, and the numbers didn't change. Chris decided it was time to move from expectations to compelling consequences. He hired a private investigator to follow the six individuals with the lowest numbers. On the first day of surveillance, the PI called Chris and said, "You're not going to believe this. The guy's been in a lingerie store at the mall for hours." A few days later he reported, "You've got a guy setting up a hot dog stand for three hours a day."

These guys were sinners, and it was obvious to Chris what he needed to do. He called them in one by one and terminated them. And since each of them had driven to the office in one of the company vehicles, Chris had taxicabs lined up outside to take them home.

He did the right thing. But he also suspected that he was now operating from a trust deficit with his save-ables. He was an unknown to them, and rumors were swirling about his use of a private investigator. Was employee surveillance Chris's standard operating procedure?

Chris decided to call everyone together again to talk about what had happened. "I thought they might stone me to death, but they listened. I reminded them about our conversations and about what I expected. I laid out the facts about how nothing had improved. I told them about the private investigator. They roared their disapproval. I said, 'I am just telling you the way it is. The results speak for themselves. I think you know we did the right thing. We got rid of the guys who were tarnishing your reputations.'"

Then he said, "From now on, let's look forward. We have great opportunities, and I think a lot of the ideas for how to take advantage of them could and should come from you guys."

"So here's what we're going to do," he said. "I'll take five guys out for a steak dinner once a month, and I'll pick up the check, including your first two beers. But the agenda is yours. If you want to talk about sports all night, we'll talk about sports. If you want to talk about the company, we can do that, too."

Chris tells us that he learned a lot from those dinners. And he's confident the guys learned he wasn't a bad guy—just an honest one trying to help lead them toward results. That's not all. In one of the sessions, an employee told him, "We arrive at these jobs, and there's a valve broken and the customer says, 'Why don't you guys just fix it?' And we're supposed to say, 'No, you've got to fix it. We just meter. Here's your 10-day shutoff notice.' But the thing is, I know how to fix it. We could be making money on this." Chris and his team implemented the idea and turned it into a million-dollar business. Not a bad return on investment on Chris's efforts to become someone the guys could relate to.

Another thing author Robert Cialdini observed is: "We like people who are similar to us. This fact seems to hold true whether the similarity is in the area of opinions, personality traits, background, or lifestyle."

This explains how it came to be that Dean Edwards, chief procurement officer at Kaiser Permanente, unintentionally raised the credibility of his high expectations as a result of his efforts to impress his father-in-law. "As someone who married up, I am often conscious of making a good impression on my in-laws, though I suspect that I often fall short," Dean, who is British, told us. "So on a holiday when they were here in the States, I took it upon myself to organize a visit for my father-in-law to come out to one of our facilities. And our employees there really did me proud. They blew his socks off with their capabilities, the level of engagement, and the interest and enthusiasm that he was able to contrast with other workforces he'd experienced in the U.K."

Dean's father-in-law went home and related his experience to his wife, who is now more confident that her daughter's husband does in fact have a proper job to support his family. After the holiday break, Dean shared the experience with a few of his people, and it instantly became a bit of folklore. "Apparently, lots of people can identify with the desire to impress their in-laws," Dean says sheepishly. "On the other hand," he adds, "I was grateful that the story conveyed my genuine appreciation to these folks—what they do, how they stand up and present themselves, and the pride they have in doing their jobs."

Of course, none of the things we're talking about here are at all useful if they're inauthentic. People can smell contrivance from a mile away.

Indeed, it is more credible to be authentically bad than inauthentically good. We share this coaching point with leaders who are thinking about using blogs, Twitter, or the like to increase visibility and engagement. It's a lesson that came out of Howard Dean's 2004 presidential campaign. People remember that campaign because of it's pioneering use of social media. But the truth is, says Joe Trippi, who managed the campaign, that "Howard Dean couldn't blog if his life depended on it." Joe learned this only after he arranged for Howard to step in as a guest blogger for Larry Lessig, a Stanford professor and influential blogger, who was planning to take a vacation.

"We let Howard be Howard, so we didn't change a thing," Joe told us. "He came on the blog and wrote, essentially, 'I'm going to start blogging now. I just wanted to say you're all terrific.'" Lessig's blogging community went nuts. They thought it was ridiculous and said so in the comments. And so Howard went back and wrote, "No, no. I really mean it, you're all terrific," which made them even more enraged. A commenter wrote, "I knew his staff would be ghostwriting this garbage, but it's like they're on autoreply."

At this point, Joe jumped on and said, "This is Joe Trippi. I'm the campaign manager, and if we were ghostwriting this stuff, don't you think we'd do a better job of it?" David Weinberger, one of the fathers of blogging, immediately wrote on another blog, "One of the most authentic moments in campaign history just happened on the Internet. Howard Dean really is typing these words. He really has just jumped in to try to blog for the first time." All of a sudden, everybody realized it was real. In other words, it was so bad it had to be real.

"This is one of the things that really jump-started the Dean phenomenon because suddenly it was authentic," Joe says. "There wasn't anything fake or phony about it. People started realizing, 'Hey, he is human like the rest of us,' and remembering the first time they had commented on a blog, maybe without completely understanding the medium. People get that."

Employees will see your expectations for high performance as more credible if they see you as someone who is familiar, authentic, and real. Of course, what's even more compelling is if they see *your relationship with them* as authentic and real. This is what Carlos Nieva, an executive with Alcatel-Lucent in Spain, believes and practices.

"I am very demanding. I ask my people to bring everything to their jobs every day. Their brain. Their heart. Their soul," Nieva says. "And yet companies cannot guarantee 'employment for life' anymore. But I can guarantee that I will be committed to them for life, no matter where they are—at a competitor, with a customer, with their own business—whatever it is."

He continues, "When we get real commitment from people, we can deliver more results. But I can't ask for real commitment if we don't have a real relationship. And if we have a real relationship, that doesn't change the minute you go somewhere else. You are still the same human being, right? I am still committed to your success even after you leave my team."

PART 2

PROVEN STRATEGIES FOR CREATING COMPELLING CONSEQUENCES

✓ Reward what you want to see more of . . . and stop tolerating what you don't (Chapter 6).

✓ Use the other f-word to tap hidden sources of motivation (Chapter 7).

✓ Wield your biggest stick: the power to take things away (Chapter 8).

✓ When you have no authority, use increased confidence and reduced anxiety as your consequence currency (Chapter 9).

REWARD WHAT YOU WANT TO SEE MORE OF . . . AND STOP TOLERATING WHAT YOU DON'T

Whether dealing with monkeys, rats, or human beings," management professor Steven Kerr wrote in 1975, "it is hardly controversial to state that most organisms seek information concerning what activities are rewarded and then seek to do (or at least pretend to do) these things, often to the virtual exclusion of activities not rewarded." The implication? If you want your people to do some particular thing, that's the thing you'd better reward. It's folly, Kerr said, to "reward A while hoping for B."[1]

But three decades later, the problem persists, as Kerr observes in his latest book.[2] Organizations want long-term performance, he notes, but they reward employees who achieve quarterly targets. So what they get, predictably, is short-term thinking and number gaming. Or they want teamwork and cooperation but reward only individual goal attainment, leading, predictably, to unproductive competition.

The phenomenon isn't limited to organizational reward systems, of course. For example, we hope for medical cures, but the U.S. health care system rewards procedures. So, predictably, we get a system in which providers focus on performing many procedures. Another example: For many years, Major League Baseball hoped players would avoid steroids—while it handsomely rewarded performance and failed to put in place testing or an accountability system with any teeth. Now every month comes the revelation that a top player of the recent era has been tied to "doping." None of this should surprise anyone. As writer Matthew Yglesias notes: "What kind of big-time baseball star would willingly eschew a performance-enhancing substance whose use was widespread among his teammates and competitors and which there was no serious policy in place to prevent? It would have to be someone who wasn't taking his baseball skills all that seriously."[3] Baseball came to be defined by what it tolerated. The same is true of many organizations.

Rewarding One Thing While Expecting "Good People" to Do Something Else: Why the U.S. Health Care System Is Messed Up

By George Halvorson, CEO, Kaiser Permanente*

We all like to think of our caregivers as good people—trying very hard to do the right thing. That is, I believe, actually very true. Our care providers are good people, all trying to do the right thing—but a bit more specifically, everyone is doing the "billable right thing." If it isn't billable, it isn't happening, successfully. Preventing a health care crisis is not billable. Care linkages are not billable. So care linkages do not happen.

So what do we actually pay for in health care today? These are the bare facts: We have over 9,000 billing codes for individual health care procedures, services, and separate units of care. There is not one single billing code for patient improvement. There is also not one single billing code for a cure. Providers have a huge economic incentive to do a lot of procedures. They have no economic incentive to actually make us better. The economic incentive score is 9,000 to 0—process versus results. Results get 0.

So what does the largest health care economy in the world produce? Cures? No. Cures aren't a billable event. Systematic health improvement? No. Health improvement is also not a billable event. No one buys it, so no one sells it.

Procedures are, however, easily billable—so our caregivers produce huge numbers of procedures. We generally pay very well for procedures in this country. In response, caregivers produce constantly expanding volumes of individual units of care. Our caregivers sell procedures one by one, and caregivers get paid for doing each procedure—with no portion of that pay ever based on actual results or success of that procedure. So the economic focus of care-givers is, of course, on individual, billable services. We can't blame providers for having that focus. That's the way providers get paid. So, of course, providers focus on the specific pieces of work that actually create payment. That provider focus on billable events needs to be there or providers will not survive in today's health care economy as economic units.

Take asthma—one of the five chronic diseases—as an example. No one pays providers to reduce either the level or the volume of asthma crises. Providers are, however, paid a lot of money to take care of an asthma patient who is in a crisis. Hospitals, in fact, make very nice profits off each asthma patient in a crisis who is admitted to the hospital. Hospitals make absolutely no money from an educated, enlightened, and personally empowered asthma patient who recognizes his or her symptoms at an early stage and then takes the steps necessary to avoid an emergency room visit or a hospitalization.

*Excerpted with permission from Halvorson's book, *Health Care Reform Now!*

Machiavelli and *The Music Man*

You know you've got a good reward system, Kerr writes, if "it gets you what you want." If that's not the case, don't blame your employees; blame your reward system. "The bad news" for leaders, he says, "is that you are responsible for the dysfunctional behaviors that so bother you."[4]

This is a message that leaders don't always want to hear, as we can attest.

"Wow, I didn't realize before that our people in the call center have so little integrity," said one of our clients. We had just briefed him on the results of the Conditions of Accountability Assessment he'd hired us to conduct. He wanted to understand why customer satisfaction had declined precipitously. We learned why easily: The firm rewarded reps for productivity, which it measured with just one variable—the number of calls handled. To make their numbers, reps blazed through as many incoming calls as possible. When they encountered a customer with a time-consuming problem, reps transferred them to another rep or—in some cases—"accidentally" hung up on them.

"Yeah," we said. "We understand your disappointment. But we think we're going to have more success coming up with a solution if we don't frame this as an 'integrity' problem but as a 'consequences' problem. That will require lining up your reward system more closely with the behaviors you want to see."

He wasn't ready to hear that. "You're making it sound like it's my fault that my people aren't accountable," he said. "Those people just need to get with the program."

We hear that a lot: "People *just need to* . . . [fill in the blank with whatever it is they're supposed to do]." Unfortunately,

"People just need to . . ." is not a solution. It's an aspiration without an action plan, kind of like the "think system" touted by Harold Hill—the traveling music teacher/con man in the *The Music Man.* "Professor" Hill would convince people to buy instruments, relying on the "think system" to learn to play them. Since Hill couldn't actually teach music, his grift was to create an illusion just long enough to collect his money and get out of town. In the real world, there's no marching band at the end of such a charade. As Machiavelli wrote in *The Prince*, "He who neglects what *is* done for what *ought to be* done, sooner effects his ruin than his preservation."

So what's the alternative? In the rest of this chapter, we'll elaborate the three simple coaching points on this topic that we frequently push to clients:

- Reward what you want to see more of.
- Stop tolerating what you don't.
- Eliminate "rewards" that aren't.

Reward What You Want to See More Of

When you find out your reward system isn't giving you what you need, you can't make excuses or hope things will change magically. You've got to take action. Here are some stories of leaders who've done just that.

"Long-Term Greedy" at Goldman Sachs

Steven Kerr, who has obviously influenced our thinking on the topic of reward systems, happens to be a senior advisor at Goldman Sachs. As you may recall, that's the financial services firm we glorified in an earlier chapter for its history of putting into practice its former managing director Gus Levy's maxim of being "greedy . . . but long-term greedy." Operating from that perspective, Goldman Sachs seldom suffered from the myopia that inflicted most of its competitors, and that was a big part of what made the firm so special.

Until, that is, the company became like everybody else.

In the publicly traded firms on Wall Street (of which Goldman Sachs was one), "you were paid [in recent years] according to (more or less) your profits or fee generation, regardless of the outcome, down the road, of the deals you did or the loans you made or the assets you took on," according to writer Nick Paumgarten. "You had an incentive to generate inflated or ephemeral gains and, often, little incentive not to." He adds: "The amazing thing about the piggishness of the last decade is that, in a certain light, most people, according to the strictures of their self-interest (whether enlightened or not), behaved rationally."[5] So, as Kerr might say, don't blame greedy employees; blame the reward system.

Toward that end, Goldman Sachs' chief executive officer (CEO), Lloyd Blankfein, has since acknowledged that "we participated in the market euphoria and failed to raise a responsible voice" in the lead-up to the financial crisis.[6] The collapse of long-term greedy required the firm to take a $10 billion government bailout—which it has since repaid. "We believe that repayment of the government's investment is a strong sign of progress and one measure of the ability to recover from the crisis," Blankfein said in a letter to congressional leaders. "But real stability can return only if our industry accepts that certain practices were unhealthy and not in the long-term interests of individual institutions and the financial system as a whole."

In other words, he wants to get back into the business of rewarding "long-term greedy." And the good news is that Blankfein appears to be backing up his words—Goldman Sachs isn't just hoping for it; it's going to reward it. In May 2009, Blankfein—presumably acting on advice from Kerr— instituted new compensation practices. Some highlights:

- To avoid misaligning compensation and performance, the firm will use guaranteed employment contracts only in exceptional circumstances (e.g., for new hires) and avoid multiyear guarantees entirely.
- The firm commits that cash compensation in a single year will never be so much as to overwhelm the value ascribed to longer-term stock incentives that can be realized only through longer-term responsible behavior.
- The firm will subject equity awards to vesting and other restrictions over an extended period of time. This allows for forfeiture or a "clawback" in the event that an employee's conduct or judgment results in a restatement of the firm's financial statements or other significant harm to the firm's business. The firm also can use the clawback in response to any individual misconduct that

results in legal or reputational harm. And equity delivery schedules continue to apply after an individual has left the firm.

- The firm commits to evaluate an employee's outsized gain, just like an outsized loss, in the context of the cumulative record of that individual's risk judgments.

This is exactly what it will take to restore a culture of "long-term greedy." Of course, it would have been far better to have never forgotten Levy's maxim in the first place. According to another well-known saying at Goldman Sachs, "Our assets are our people, capital, and reputation. If any of these is ever diminished, the last is the most difficult to restore." How true! As of this writing, Goldman Sachs' stock price has rebounded faster than its reputation. According to a trader at a rival firm, "The guys at Goldman are still feared . . . but the mystique they had is gone."[7]

Rewarding What You Want to See: Accurate Sales Forecasting at Cypress Communications

When Steve Schilling took over as president and CEO of Cypress Communications, sales were in decline, and the executive team was cracking down on salespeople. The weekly reviews were like interrogations: "Are you gonna close the deal this month? Are you sure you're gonna get it? You're really gonna have to get that done, you know?" So sales reps would show up to those meetings with numbers that looked good, even if they were bogus. "They'd just tell management what they wanted to hear," Steve says, "because they were in job-preservation mode. We were *hoping* for accurate forecasts, but unintentionally *rewarding* inflated ones."

So he was incredulous when he heard the executives talking to the board about how the pipeline had grown bigger and bigger, month over month, and was continuing to grow, and "if we close *x* percent of it, then we'll get to these numbers."

"That analysis only works if there's any validity to the pipeline," Steve said. "And if all we're doing is scaring people into making the pipeline bigger, they'll throw in every piece of junk they can find."

As a result, net sales performance was far below plan, there was no clear visibility into the actual funnel, monthly forecasts were not met—and Steve and his team had no clarity about the future performance of the company.

"So we got rid of all that silliness," Steve says. He started by asking his people to forecast with absolute honesty and assured them that all past sins would be forgiven. But he knew that wasn't enough. To move the pipeline as close to reality as possible, Cypress implemented what the company called the "Blood Oath" forecast. Steve explains: "We ask our sales managers for the 30-day forecast they're committing to and then have them pledge that they've actually talked to each one of those prospects to help validate that their folks are on track. The reps know that if they're going to put something in their forecasts for the next 30 days, their managers are going to speak to each and every prospect and validate it appropriately. So, now, if they try to inflate their numbers, everyone is going to know about it."

It changed the forecasts—and the conversations around sales opportunities. "We're now performing at 100 percent improvement over our previous production and delivering consistently within 10 percent of our monthly forecast," Steve told us.

Equally important, operations now can make real plans based on the sales forecasts, which makes them much more effective. But that's not the only benefit. "Recently, an important deal that we'd forecasted derailed as the month was coming to a close," Steve says. "So we called our sales managers and said, 'Look, we're going to be short this month, so what can we move up?' We made it clear [that] we weren't looking to punish anyone—we just wanted to solve the problem. We had people look at what they'd forecast to see what they were close to closing. We looked for incentives to give them for closing sooner than expected. We got everyone on board to try to help move those things along."

Sure enough, salespeople found deals they could accelerate, and Cypress hit its number for the month within $1,000. "We were able to do this only because the forecast was real, and we knew what our real opportunities were. And it was a really exciting thing to watch because the sales organization now takes a lot of pride in their forecast too, in addition to making their numbers."

Abandon the Hope Method, All Ye Who Enter Here . . . and Take Action Instead

Here are a couple of other interesting examples of leaders rewarding what they want to see more of . . . instead of just hoping for it:

> We're working to break down silos here. We had too much "white space" between functions. So we're implementing incentives that reward cross-functional behavior and achievement of cross-functional goals. And whenever I find an opportunity for a problem that comes to my attention, I assign people from at least two different functions to work together on it. Not because it is necessarily the most efficient way of solving a problem but because it promotes— requires—cooperation and communication across boundaries, which for now is really needed . . . until this is more natural for people.
>
> —Bob Walton, Division President, Qualcomm Enterprise Services

> One of our metrics of success is how many of our people who have been rated poorly for performance move out of that rating into solid levels of performance in the subsequent 12 months. It is a very

important metric for us. Most people would say, "Drop them." Our greater pride is rehabilitating them. So, that is where we spend a lot of our energy. It is not always successful. . . . we've had to let go of some people. But I think that one of the reasons we have tremendous crew member retention—even though we are very demanding—is because people realize that we view it as our problem when somebody fails here.

—Jack Brennan, Chairman and former CEO, Vanguard

Note: Brennan's strategy only works because the company is hard core about hiring; the company has a lot of confidence in the quality of the people it brings on board.

. . . And Stop Tolerating What You Don't

"Reward what you want to see more of" has a corollary: "Stop tolerating what you don't." Here we'll share some stories of leaders who have put this principle into practice—or wished they had.

Our friend, Roger Mann, and his family had a garden behind their house in Arusha, Tanzania, where they raised vegetables. A local gardener tended it from Monday to Saturday. On Sundays, when the gardener wasn't there, monkeys stole from the garden. Roger asked one of his friends for advice. "No problem," he said. "I'll bring my gun over and shoot one of them. It will scare the others away."

But Roger didn't like that idea—it seemed so distasteful—so he asked around for other options. Someone suggested that they trap one of the monkeys and hang a cowbell on him. "The noise will frighten away all the other monkeys." So Roger found someone who was very clever to design a trap and hired a carpenter to build it. The next Sunday they loaded it with bait and very quickly trapped a monkey. And then, with a bunch of help, they put a cowbell around the monkey's neck.

It didn't work: The vegetable thievery continued. "And it was annoying," Roger recalls, "because we could hear this monkey running around with a cowbell around his neck, and it didn't seem to bother any of the other monkeys. In fact, I suspect it became a source of prestige for him!"

Again, one of Roger's friends offered to come and shoot one of the monkeys, but again he resisted. Another neighbor theorized that if they trapped a monkey and painted him white, the others would think they were seeing a ghost, and it would scare them all away. So Roger trapped another monkey and painted him white with a good oil-based paint. Same outcome: The other monkeys didn't care. If anything, they found it intriguing.

The next Sunday, Roger's friend—the one with the gun—came over. Together they crouched in the garden. When a monkey showed up in the branches above, Roger's friend took aim, fired one shot, and the dead monkey dropped to the ground. "We never had another problem with monkeys stealing from our garden," Roger says.

On the advice of legal counsel, we"ll hasten to emphasize that this is an *allegory*. We don't advocate shooting anyone. The moral that we want you take away from this story is that sometimes you've got to take unpleasant action to confront bad behavior—and it's a mistake to delay it or rationalize it away. When we see our clients doing it—for example, turning a blind eye to a top performer's indiscretions or hanging onto an employee who everyone knows is beyond redemption and is sucking energy from the system but whose termination would require messy paperwork— we call it "painting a monkey" in Roger's honor.

Randy Gier, chief consumer officer at Dr. Pepper/Snapple, learned his own lesson about painting monkeys early in his career when he continued to tolerate an employee who was delivering results, but not in the right way. "What's worse," Randy says, "is that I promoted him."

He explains: "I thought I could manage it. I thought: We'll promote him, and then we'll talk to him, and we'll tell him that his negative behavior is not going to work anymore: 'Now that you're promoted, you're going to have to operate differently.'" And guess what? All the employee heard was, 'I got promoted. I must be very good, so I'm going to do more of it.' "

Randy continues: "You end up needing a bigger two-by-four later on to hit them on the side of the head and say, 'Did you not hear me?' Or you end up firing them. Only now, you've got someone you just invested in and promoted. And you've sent all the wrong messages to your organization. They think, 'They promoted that guy? Don't they get that he's a jerk?' They don't believe you couldn't have seen it, since everyone else does."

That's the downside of tolerating the behavior you don't want to see. One of the unexpected upsides of deciding that you're not going to tolerate bad behavior is that sometimes even the person you're confronting is happy about it.

Doug Hawkins currently directs international trade relations for Wyeth, but early in his career he worked in Geneva for a very senior-level diplomat. The diplomat, who had 400 reports, had a very casual way of operating. His assistant, who was French, had little respect for him, and she showed it.

She started taking longer and longer coffee breaks. From 15 minutes . . . to 20, 25, 30 minutes . . . until she got up to an hour. Finally, this very seasoned diplomat and manager had had enough. He said, "I need you back in the office. I need you to attend to the work we pay you to do, and you cannot take these very long coffee breaks. I need you here. I expect you to be here." She promptly related the story to Doug, adding: "Finally, he is acting like a real boss."

Our colleague Gareth Powell tells a similar story. He brought a software developer onto his team who was likable

but very easily distracted. If this employee heard an interesting fragment of conversation, he stopped programming
and went to join the discussion. Then he'd return to his desk
to do a Google search on whatever the conversation had
been about.

But he didn't seem very happy because he wasn't getting
much accomplished. So Gareth called him out on his lack of
productivity. Not only did his performance improve, but he
also seemed relieved and pleased that someone was holding
him accountable.

Before we move on, we need to share this one caveat:
It's not meaningful to say that you're going to stop tolerating bad behavior among those who lack the *capability*
to give you the good behavior you want to see instead—
because it won't stop the sinning. By way of illustration,
one of Gregg's clients, Nina, was having some challenges
with a new hire, Jason, and asked Gregg to coach him. But
then Nina called Gregg and said she'd changed her mind.
"Jason's a senior director, and I just need him to start acting
like one," she said. "At the senior director level, you should
be able to. . . . " And Nina proceeded to describe a variety of
things that a senior director ought to be able to do but that
Jason apparently could not. "I don't want to have to pay for
coaching for something he should already know how to do."
And, she added, "I'm just taking your advice about not tolerating the behavior I don't want to see more of."

Gregg's feedback was

- You hired him.
- Given that you hired him, what responsibility are you taking for vetting Jason's skill sets and competencies?
- Maybe this was a selection mistake. So you can move him out. Or keep him. But if it's the latter, why compound the mistake by withholding the coaching, feedback, direction, and support that theoretically he shouldn't need—but clearly does? How is that possibly going to work?

The Power of Consequences

By Mike Rawlings, former president of Pizza Hut

I was asked by the mayor of Dallas to be the "Homeless Czar." One of my strategies was to create the MetroDallas Homeless Alliance, an independent organization that could work across government and organizational boundaries. So I went out and hired a CEO, someone who was familiar with working with government and with the nonprofit sector. Very bright guy with a good heart. But he had never worked with someone like me.

Our different backgrounds showed when we created objectives for the year. He started with a laundry list and with the mind-set that the thicker the document is, the better it is. I wrote his objectives on a cocktail napkin—four or five big ones.

At the end of the year, we sat down to evaluate his performance. First, I let him grade himself. And then I graded him. One of his objectives was a plan for permanent housing for the homeless. Very complex to do. But we had put it into his objectives and set a deadline for the end of the year. It really needed to be done. It wasn't. I asked for a chief financial officer (CFO) to be hired. At the end of the year, it wasn't done. There were a lot of reasons why these things weren't done, but they weren't done. As a result, he did not get his full bonus. He wasn't happy.

So going into what is now our second year, we still had unfinished objectives from the year before, plus a new set of objectives. This year, coming out of the gate, he jumped all over the objectives and took them very, very seriously. Permanent, supportive housing plan? Almost done. CFO? Hired. And the year's not over. Just about everything he has to do this year has been done, and done well.

Once he realized that this was not government bureaucracy, that I was serious, and that there were real consequences for nonperformance, he's been great.

Eliminate "Rewards" That Aren't

Rewards that no one really wants won't help your cause. In our experience, they come in three varieties:

- The Good Citizen Award or its equivalent

- The Treadmill Award
- The Bali Punch

The Good Citizen Award

When Jeff was in fourth grade, he won the "good citizen award" after a classmate thoroughly beat him up at recess. The contest was so one-sided that the teacher who broke it up assumed that Jeff was refusing to fight back—hence the award. (Alas, he was at that time merely a weakling.) The schoolyard shame and taunting associated with winning such a dubious honor were far worse than that associated with getting pummeled.

Our friend Ed Gwozda, who works in big pharma, endured a similar experience in a corporate setting. "Some years ago," he recalls, "my sales team won four 'Out of the Box' awards. One of my guys took first place because he found a way to link mental health professionals with community members. Because I redefined sales territories—based on customer needs and type of business, and not just by geography—I won the sales manager award." Unfortunately, he operated in a culture where leaders fancied themselves innovative. But the truth was that what they valued even more was keeping things just as they were. "So along with the awards came some unwanted recognition. Our unusual thinking branded us as 'out there,'" he says. And that made it harder for his team to work with others to get things done. "You can probably imagine the subsequent impact on my team's 'out of the box' thinking," he adds. That was the first and last year they gave out "creativity" awards.

The Treadmill Award

The challenge of the videogame industry is to create a great entertainment experience and a high-quality software program within the constraints of a tight 12- to 36-month period. The last month of a project—called the *finaling phase*—is often the toughest. "I have always said that the most productive days of our lives are those with our backs against the wall," says Rusty Rueff, executive vice president of human resources for Electronic Arts. "But I learned some tough lessons about what happens when you let the 'backs-against-the-wall days' drift into 12 to 15 hours a day, seven days a week, week after week, over multiple months."

He came to realize that management was administering the Treadmill Award, continuously ratcheting up expectations without relief. "Every time they met a deadline, we tightened the deadlines and asked them to do more. What seemed like a positive consequence—the excitement of delivering a hit videogame to the market—became very negative," he says. "We were rewarding their success with negative consequences: higher workloads and longer hours. All the intentions were right. But it couldn't work long term. In fact, the whole system began to backfire." To his credit, Rusty has helped to lead the effort to rethink reward systems in the industry to incent high performance in sustainable ways.

The Bali Punch

By far the worst *award that isn't* is the Bali Punch. One of Jeff's brothers, Jeremy, is a professor of musicology, and a couple of years ago he spent a few months in Bali working with gamelan musicians. In one of his e-mails home, he wrote

> An old man always hangs out at our rehearsals. For some reason, he and I ended up sitting next to each other once, and he started talking to me, and I looked confused, and he cackled and elbowed me in the ribs. This has become our routine. Each day I sit next to him, he talks to me, I grin and shake my head, and he cackles and hits me. Finally, someone translated for me. Apparently he was saying, "I'm an old man, so I don't have to worry about taking care of kids or working. So I just go to the temple and pray and think about God all day long. What? You don't speak Indonesian? You're so stupid! I'm going to hit you now! Ha!"

A similar routine plays out in many of the organizations we've studied. Many managers seem to say to their top performers (their saints), "I don't have the discipline to replace or hold my poor performers (sinners) accountable. But you keep accepting every new assignment I give you. You're so stupid! I'm going to give you even more work to do now. Ha!"

To date, we've counted at least 14 organizations where this perverse phenomenon—"rewarding" top performers with more work to compensate for poor performance management—occurs with enough frequency that employees refer to it sardonically as "The ____ Reward," filling in the blank with the name of the company. It's dark humor, to be sure, because it's not sustainable and eventually will drive away your saints and kill your culture.

One of the places where you can encounter the Bali Punch is in the U.S. Department of Defense, where our friend Eric works. While his coworkers are taking extralong coffee breaks, feigning incompetence to avoid assignments, and working on their hobbies (one of his office mates spends his days ordering parts for classic autos), Eric picks up the slack—working extra hours.

When Eric's boss came on board, he promised there was going to be accountability. But he hasn't followed through; instead, he makes excuses. Eric's boss says, "It's not my fault"; "You need to understand where I'm coming from"; and "You shouldn't question my process." This is apparently why it's necessary for him to give Eric other people's work to do—and then micromanage him.

The problem for Eric is that the Bali Punch works on him, and it's because of how he's wired. As the eldest of nine children, he learned responsibility early, and he has a strong work ethic. After leaving home, he spent a lot of years in the Army, where the ethos is, "We do more before 8 a.m. than most people do all day." So he is constitutionally incapable of not working hard or slacking like everyone else—even though, strictly speaking, that would be the rational thing to do. But he resents the abuse, and just like Jeremy sitting next to the old man in Bali, he is looking for an opportunity to get up and walk away.

"Rewarding Development Opportunity" versus "Just More Work"

Interesting challenges are a great way to reward and develop up-and-comers. Steve Walker, a leadership development executive for a Fortune 25 company, says the key to doing this well is to take a structured approach. For people to actually learn something, you need to have

- a targeted outcome in mind
- some level of preparation
- some level of stretch or discomfort to encourage people to grow
- some time for reflection about what happened

"Without these things, people won't take anything away," he says. "While that sounds obvious, so much development activity isn't characterized by any of these things—and if that's the case, 'development opportunity' is probably just a code word for giving people more work."

CHAPTER 7

USE THE OTHER F-WORD TO TAP HIDDEN SOURCES OF MOTIVATION

Here's some good news: When it comes to creating compelling consequences, you have more options than you realize. This is so because *your greatest source of power is your ability to change how people feel.* And as a leader, you have enormous capacity to do just that among the people on whom you depend for high accountability and performance.

Before we proceed, we'll concede that this insight has provoked a negative visceral reaction in many of the leaders with whom we've shared it over the past decade or so. And we know why: In serious business settings, it's taboo to talk about *feelings*—a mushy word that evokes rainbows, unicorns, and Johnny Mathis. Our maxim "feels" like something you'd expect to see written in cross-stitch.

So we felt vindicated, our credibility bolstered, when in 2002 Daniel Kahneman won the Nobel Prize in economics. In his acceptance speech, he summarized the years of research that earned him the reward and said—albeit in academic language—pretty much what we've been saying all along.

Before we tell you specifically what Professor Kahneman said, let's refresh your memory about a term you may recall from Economics 101: *Utility* refers to the value that individuals gain from a good or experience. We make choices, according to the logic of economics, that we think will maximize our utility—taking into account our options and their relative tradeoffs. Should you buy a Lexus or a Mercedes? According to the logic of economics, you'll make the choice based on which option you believe maximizes utility. Will your top performer continue to work for you or take the calls of every headhunter around? According to the logic of economics, she'll make that important economic choice based on which option she thinks maximizes her utility.

One of Kahneman's breakthrough ideas was that people frequently make choices that don't conform to the logic of traditional economics, which for 275 years has tended to discount the importance of emotion and feelings in economic decision making. Kahneman, a psychologist who never took an economics course, says that's a mistake. Why? Because "[u]tility cannot be divorced from emotion. . . . A theory of choice that completely ignores feelings . . . leads to prescriptions that do not maximize the utility of outcomes *as they are actually experienced*" (emphasis ours).

In other words, most of the time we don't actually experience utility based on calculations about objective criteria of what we *should* value. Rather, we experience utility based on how our economic choices *actually make us feel.* You pick either a Lexus or a Mercedes over a more "rational" option—that is, a cheaper car that works just as well and gets better mileage—because of the way it makes you *feel.* Your top performer chooses to stick with you over another job that would pay her more money because of the way her current job makes her *feel.* Respected. Appreciated. Affiliated. Successful. Purposeful. Autonomous. Secure. Some combination of the preceding. Or maybe something else entirely.

To recap what we've covered so far, we told you that your greatest source of power for creating compelling consequences is your ability to change how people feel. And in case our assertion felt a little too "New Agey," we invoked a Nobel Prize–winning economist to corroborate it. Now let's look at its practical implications. In the rest of this chapter, we will (1) help you expand the list of compelling consequences you can use in the f-word economy in which you operate in order to motivate your people to do what you need them to do, (2) offer insights into the emotional algorithms that often come into play when your employees are experiencing and responding to rewards and consequences, and (3) explain why tough times can be the best times to change how your people feel. Equipped with this information, you can make smarter choices about how to put your greatest source of power to its most effective use—so that you can compete more effectively for your people's performance and discretionary effort.

You Have More Consequence Capital than You Think

When we're talking to a group of leaders for the first time, we'll often ask them to take 30 seconds to come up with a list of the consequences (both positive and negative) they can use to motivate people to do what they want them to do. A typical group will generate a list that looks something like this:

Compensation
Bonuses
"Thanks"
Time off
Prizes (vacations, etc.)
Termination
Status/title
Operational resources (budget, headcount, etc.)

Administrative support

Developmental resources (arranging for a mentor, getting them an executive coach)

Then we'll ask, "Is this a pretty good list? Does it include most of the consequences you have available to you?" And they'll usually add a few more things and then say, "Yes, this is a pretty good list." Next, we'll tell them about their greatest source of power (and cite Daniel Kahneman). That changes the frame. Now they're thinking about all the ways they can influence or change the way their people feel. And the "pretty good" list no longer seems adequate. So then we give them another minute to add to the list. Here are the kinds of things that the typical group of leaders will add to the list of compelling consequences—ways they can change how their people feel:

Acceptance

Public recognition/credit

Responsiveness to their needs/requests

Time and attention

Inclusion in activities, decisions, etc.

Privileged information

Familiarity (knowing their name and something about them)

Acknowledgment ("Hi," eye contact)

Consultation (seek their feedback and advice)

Buzz (third-party compliments, creating positive
  folklore)
Partnering with them
Staying out of their way
Introductions
Visibility (upward and across the organizations, to
  clients, etc.)
Conveniences
Free time
Freedom to fail/controlled failure (for high performers)
Absolution (past mistakes forgotten)
New experiences

A couple of things to note: First, you can turn most of
these positive consequences into negative consequences just
by taking them away or not providing them in the first place.
Second, the point here *isn't* to suggest that this is a comprehensive list of compelling consequences. Such a list will differ
from leader to leader and organization to organization. And
honestly, we hear new ideas all the time. Our key coaching
point here is: You have lots of capacity to change the way
people feel. So you have more options than you think to
motivate people to do the stuff you need them to do. Give
it some thought. Make a list of the ways you can influence
the way your people feel. And then match it up with the list
you made after reading Chapter 6—the things you want to
see more of and therefore need to reward more consistently.
And the things you want to no longer plan to tolerate and
therefore need to meet with negative consequences. Then,

with no excuses, take action to create more accountability and higher performance.

Emotional Algorithms: Five Principles for the F-Word Economy

When we mentioned Daniel Kahneman earlier in this chapter, you might have recognized his name. That's probably because it's appearing more and more often in the business press these days as executives are beginning to discover that behavioral economics—the field that Kahneman helped to establish—has profound implications for leadership. Drawing heavily (but not entirely) on Kahneman's research, here are five principles that will help you to put your greatest source of power—your ability to change how people feel—to its most effective use to create compelling consequences and drive accountability.

First Principle: You Can't Measure the Utility of a Consequence—Its Effective Value—in Absolute Terms: It's All Relative to Expectations and Social Comparison

What the heck does this mean? Let's use this example: What's the motivating value of a $10,000 year-end bonus? Well, it depends on three relative comparisons.

The first comparison is: *How does the reward compare with what the recipient expects?* As neuroscientists are learning, the dopamine neurons in our heads, which help us to make decisions about what to keep doing or stop doing, respond not to rewards or their absence but to "deviations from expectations." What's more, violations of expectations trigger powerful emotional responses.[1] Thus, if you give the $10,000 year-end bonus to an employee who got a $5,000 bonus last year and has worked hard to improve his performance in the past 12 months, there's a good chance the bonus you just issued will help to motivate him to continue to improve his performance and give you discretionary effort. On the other hand, if you give the $10,000 bonus to an employee who got $25,000 last year, and if you neglect in advance to explain the difference, she's probably going to walk away. And that's why we say that just because something is very easy to measure—in this case, a $10,000 bonus measured in hard dollars—it doesn't mean the measurement is meaningful.

When we ask employees to tell us about a positive consequence that they found to be especially motivating, they frequently will describe a reward that was deserved but "random" or unexpected. For example, one day some years ago airline executive Lois Oller called her direct reports to her office for an unscheduled short meeting. The group had been working long hours in response to a new marketing program. The lead time to implement was ambitious and, "if the truth be told, unreasonable," Lois concedes. "Our team responded to the challenge, and I wanted them to know that I recognized their Herculean effort." When they arrived, they saw a large hat, staged in the middle of Lois's desk. In the hat were small pieces of paper with upcoming dates on them. Lois passed the hat and asked everyone to pick one. Then she said, "I want all of you to know how much I appreciate the effort you put in recently and what we've accomplished for this company. Your hard work does not go unnoticed. As something above and beyond the usual rewards we do around here, I just want you to take a day off on the date you selected." Her team talked about it for years. The motivational value of this "random reward" far exceeded the cost to the company in extra days off.

Of course, when your competitors are flailing in the f-word economy—not making their people feel the way they want to feel—it can give you a competitive advantage in attracting top talent (without having to pay them more money). Shortly after Terry Mullen took the helm at Lincoln Financial Distributors, he was inundated with résumés from a competitor. As a professional courtesy, Terry called his counterpart at the other company and said, "Hey, I just want to give you a heads up. I don't know what's going on over there, but I've received all these unsolicited résumés." To Terry's surprise, the competitor said, " 'F' them. If they don't want to be here, screw 'em." Then, six months later, he called Terry back and asked him to stop taking all his people. Terry explained that people kept coming over and that he hadn't made a single proactive call. "In a three-year period, that company crashed because they treated their people so poorly and they all left," Terry recalls. "All in all, we took about 80 people from them. My biggest fear was that they'd bring their negative culture with them. But everyone who came was very grateful to be in a culture where they felt more appreciated." Terry and his firm changed the way those people felt—and they've rewarded him with loyalty and high performance.

The second relative comparison is: *What are other people getting?* A $5,000 bonus will produce a stronger influence on the recipient if he knows that most of his peers received a bonus half that size. But, if he learns that some of his peers received $7,500 for what he perceives to be similar or inferior performances, the motivating power of that same $5,000 disappears, and he feels insulted.

Of course, perceptions of fairness come into play when we make social comparisons. In fact, it appears we're wired to make very sensitive calibrations about whether something is fair. According to researchers, we process "concepts of fairness . . . in the insular cortex, or insula, which is also the seat of emotional reactions."[2] This goes a long way toward explaining some of the things we repeatedly find in our accountability research, specifically the high levels of resentment that employees feel when

- *They perceive that the organization tolerates poor performers.* Across organizations, we find that employees are highly conscious of what leaders do about "dead weight." This finding usually confuses those leaders who are operating from the assumption that employees would be disturbed by any significant use of negative consequences. We have rarely found this to be the case. Lisa Bauer, senior vice president of Hotel Operations at Royal Caribbean, is one of the leaders who gets it. "When we allow poor performers to stay, we hear about it in employee surveys," she says. "They see it as an injustice . . . and they're right."

- *They perceive that the organization actually creates positive consequences for poor performers.* In many organizations where leaders have failed to create the conditions of accountability, poorly performing employees have less work to do because they have "taught" their supervisor not to count on them.

Some leaders respond to these findings by saying (if only to us): "The people who are pissed off [because they perceive that we tolerate poor performers] should just worry about themselves and the employment deal we cut specifically with them. Let *us* decide how to deal with the poor per-formers." This argument has some logical appeal. But not much else. As Kahneman says, you should never assume that reactions governed "by the emotion of the moment will be internally coherent or even reasonable by the cooler criteria of reflective reasoning."

The third relative comparison is: *What do I already have?* Another term you may recall from Economics 101 is *declining marginal utility,* which is the idea that the more of something an individual has, the less valuable having more of it will be to that individual.[3] Financial rewards tend to exhibit declining marginal utility, as illustrated in this example: Jane started out in the mail room making $25,000 per year. At that level of compensation, a $2,000 bonus probably carried a lot of motivating influence. However, after Jane worked her way up to CEO and was drawing a $750,000 base, $2,000 was "lunch money."

Traditional forms of recognition, such as an A+ certificate that the recipient can hang on the wall of his or her cubicle, also tend to exhibit declining marginal utility. The first time an employee earns one, he or she may experience 10 f-points of utility.[4] The second time he or she gets the certificate, it goes down to a six. The third time, two. It's still valuable—just not as much. (Of course, social comparison can change the experience. If the employee has four certificates hanging on his or her wall and no one else has more than one, this could more than compensate for the declining marginal utility.)

This is one of the reasons we're big fans of using new experiences and cool challenges as a reward for performers. The more unique or novel an experience, the less vulnerable it is to declining marginal utility.

Second Principle: People Are More Sensitive to Losses than Gains

"The disutility of giving up an object is greater than the utility associated with acquiring it."[5] This is true by a factor of about 2 to 2.5, according to Kahneman. In other words, the pain of losing $100 isn't equal to the satisfaction of finding $100. The pain of that loss is more equivalent—to the extent that one can compare such things—to the joy of finding $200 to $250.

One of the practical implications of this is that, in the f-word economy, lots of leaders are unintentionally administering negative consequences—often without even knowing it. Some examples:

- You tell a junior associate that you're going to hand her control of an important account. You come back two hours later and say, "Y'know, I changed my mind." You think the net effect is zero. In the real world, though, that up-and-comer feels far worse than if you'd never said a word. Again, it's hard to attribute quantitative values, but if giving the employee the account is worth +50 f-points, then changing your mind means the employee loses at least 100.

- You decide to provide free snacks and caffeinated beverages for everyone staying late. A month later, you're surprised by how much it costs to provide the perk. Apparently, your people eat a lot of snacks. Lesson learned. Now there's an "honor" box for them to pay for their snacks. Why are they pissed about it? There were no snacks at all a month ago. Well, now you know. Buying snacks = 5 f-points. Making them pay for them = –10.

- You pass someone three levels below you in the parking lot. For some reason, you remember his name. "Hi, Sam." He beams. A week later you pass him again in the cafeteria. He greets you by name. Oh-no! You blank on his. "Oh, hi, uh . . . there." You say to yourself: "Hey, I'm battin' .500 on remembering his name. Not bad." But he walks away feeling hurt. Maybe literally. Neuroscientists who put people in magnetic resonance imaging (MRI) machines and then test their responses to certain situations have found that the brain scans of those who have just endured a social snub look a lot like the brain scans of people who've just been slapped or have just broken a bone.[6] Acknowledgment by name when it was unexpected = 200 f-points. And then forgetting it = –400.

So what are we saying? You can never change your mind or forget a name? No. But if you know this principle, it might help you to avoid some choices that create unintended negative consequences.

The upside of this principle—and it's a big upside—is that your ability to create compelling negative consequences for poor performers is not limited to writing them up or firing them, which is what many managers seem to think. There are so many other things you can take away or withdraw. Such things as prized assignments, privileged information, consultation, autonomy, and attention. "Nothing is more powerful than ignoring somebody," says executive coach Robin Abramson. For example, she recently worked with a leader who had an employee with whom he was close. The employee got sloppy in some of his assignments. He and his leader talked about it, but the bad behavior continued—until the leader stopped responding to the employee's voice-mail messages and e-mails. The employee quickly changed his ways in order to earn back his boss's attention.

Another colleague, researcher Jan Lee, recently completed a study that looked at regulatory and security-related compliance practices across dozens of companies. She identified two groups. Members of the first group complained that their company paid mostly lip service to compliance, and they felt vulnerable. When she asked members of this group to describe the negative consequences for noncompliance in their organizations, most of them said "none" or "nothing consistent." By contrast, the members of the second group of companies all reported high levels of compliance. How did they get there? When Jan asked them about negative consequences for noncompliance, most members of this group said that they take things away from noncompliers, for example, "reductions in authority," "restricting access to company resources," and "turning off network and VPN access until we get compliance."

In Chapter 8, we'll describe some other ways to leverage loss aversion to create compelling consequences.

Third Principle: Scarcity Matters

As Robert Cialdini observed in his classic treatise entitled, *Influence*,[7] "[O]pportunities seem more valuable to us when their availability is limited." He describes an experiment conducted by Stephen Worchel in which participants were handed a cookie from a jar and asked to taste it and rate its desirability. Half the participants received their cookie from a jar with nine others; the other half received an identical cookie from a jar that contained just two. "As we might expect from the scarcity principle," Cialdini says, "when the cookie was one of the only two available, it was rated more favorably than when it was one of ten." Respondents reported higher levels of desire and attributed greater value to "the cookie in short supply."

What does this mean for you? For starters, it means that what's known to be most scarce—your time and attention—are enormously valuable currencies. Do you manage them that way?

As executive coach Robin Abramson advises, "[L]eaders need to think about where they're spending their time, and what message they are sending to the rest of the organization. Spending time with your 'A' players sends the message, 'The more you perform, the more I'm interested in what you're doing, and the more I'll spend time with you.'"

Alternatively, she says, "[Y]ou need to be careful about the amount of time you spend with the people who are the biggest pains in the neck. They may be the ones who are constantly asking for it and requiring it, but focusing too much time on them actually provides positive consequences for those who screw up. And worse, it sends the message to the rest of the organization that 'You screw up and I'll spend time with you.'"

MedeFinance Chief Information Officer (CIO)/Chief Technology Officer (CTO) Dave Watson agrees; he's very conscientious about how he invests his time and attention as a scarce motivational currency. "There's the generic 'management by wandering around,' when you just go walk about, in the Australian tradition, with no particular goal other than to connect with people—see what they have to say. And it's a great way to get feedback," he says. "But there are boundaries in terms of what you can accomplish when you wander into somebody's cube, flop down in the chair, and go 'What do you do?' If they know me and know I have 5,000 people reporting to me, the immediate response is, 'Holy cow, Batman.' And not in a good way. It creates an unintended message you can't control."

Dave would rather focus his walk-abouts on the high performers. "You know Jim, over at Interface Engineering, stood up in that all-hands meeting, said some really good stuff, and I've heard good things. I'm just going to buck over and see how he's doing. 'Hey Jim, how's it going? I really appreciate your comments. You know, this change is pretty tough: Are you doing all right?'"

Another colleague, Bill Adams of management consulting firm Maxcomm, sees an increasing demand for this particular currency. "In my experience, up-and-comers are choosing between job offers less on the basis of dollars and more on the basis of how much time and attention they are going to get from their leader," he says. "For example, I talked recently with a guy who is considering a senior role.

He's trying to determine if his prospective leader will take the time to give him positive and negative feedback to ensure that his direction is clear. That's his choice point."

Of course, time and attention aren't the only things that are more valuable because they're scarce. As Jim Ryan from Lincoln Financial Distributors told us, one of the reasons their annual cruise is such a powerful motivator is its scarcity. "In two weeks, I'm going on a cruise from Lisbon to Barcelona with our top salespeople. Not many people get to go, which is what makes the trip truly special. I had five slots for top performers and two spots set aside—one for whoever the team votes to be 'MVP' and the other for a rising star. And it's really all about performance. Someone who has really worked their tail off for the past year and a half but is brand new to the organization may go over someone who has been here a long time."

The scarcity principle also applies to cool assignments. For example, when clients ask us to conduct a Conditions of Accountability Assessment and help them to determine how to act on the findings, we typically give them two options: "We can come in, collect the data, conduct the analysis, present our recommendations, and help you translate them into action, or we can partner with you to do something that's often even better: put together a team of emerging leaders who we will coach and facilitate through the process."

When we recently worked with Kaiser Permanente's chief procurement officer, Dean Edwards, he chose the latter option. "The great thing about this," Dean says, "is that even before the emerging leader team conducts the accountability assessment, we've done something useful. We've said to them, at least implicitly, 'You are valuable, and we're paying attention to you.' So we're going to give you an assignment that, besides generating useful analysis and recommendations, gives you exposure to key senior leaders in the larger organization and a unique leadership-development experience."

"It also sends a message to the rest of the organization," Dean adds: "'We are proactively focusing on people who are performing. Not just those who make noise and squeak a lot.' We also heard the concerns of people who were not selected. I was happy to know they were paying attention and looking for insights about what they might need to do to make the list next time. Message sent. Message received."

Fourth Principle: Timing Matters, So Bring Consequences Closer

Economists, psychologists, and others have long observed and studied the human tendency to prefer smaller rewards now to larger payoffs later. While it's certainly a reflection on our lack of self-discipline, there also may be a certain logic at play. Researchers have found that "massive events" such as winning the lottery have no lasting impact on happiness but that "small and frequent boosts . . . lead to improved well-being."[8]

The practical application for leaders? Bring consequences closer to get from them the greatest motivational value. Our colleague Chuck Blumenkamp, a long-time veteran of the telecom industry, learned from his experience leading teams the wisdom of adopting "a spur-of-the-moment approach" to rewards. "By that," Chuck says, "I mean connecting with people directly, looking them in the eye, shaking their hand and saying, 'That was awesome. Great job.' You stop right there and engage them in a conversation to reinforce something exemplary." What's important is (1) timeliness—as soon as you are aware of the exemplary performance—and (2) specificity—telling people exactly what they did that made the difference.

At Lincoln Financial, Terry Mullen takes a similar tack. He sits down at night to see who has had a record month. "Then I send them a quick e-mail—not a formal letter—and they know it really comes from me because it's 11 p.m.," he says. The note might say, "Hey Joe, I just saw you had a record month at $11 million. Congratulations." Terry's found that "Even a quick, private recognition seems to mean a lot to them."

At the organizational level, Terry and his team have elevated the principle of pulling consequences closer to an artform. "In our model," says Terry's colleague, Jim Ryan, "the carrot is right in front of you. It's real; it's genuine. And it benefits the team in two ways: financially and publicly. People know that if they do well, their efforts will be high-lighted now—not a year from now." We asked him and Terry to elaborate:

"Look at Wall Street's approach to retention," Terry said. "They always lose their employees at the beginning of every year. It's because of the poor payout schedule. Employees receive an annual bonus on January 15 or February 15, and right after they get it, they walk out the door."

And at Lincoln Financial? "We structure our calendar to keep employees here," Terry told us. "Let's take a look at our calendar: In January, you don't want to leave because that's when you're getting paid on December's business, which typically includes your highest commissions. In February, you don't want to leave because you have the Leader's Club trip, which the top people go to, and it's such a great location. So at this point, you may say, 'I'm just going to wait until after the trip, then I'll leave.' But then, in March, you don't want to leave because your 401k matching contribution hits. And then April, May, and June fly by, and there are cash retention payouts in July. So no one's going to leave before then, or they'd be walking away from $50,000. By fall, you've got all this momentum, and you're not going to leave because it just wouldn't make any sense to walk away from the money."

Fifth Principle: Everybody's Different

Because everyone's emotional makeup is different, the utility or motivating value of any consequence is in the eye of the beholder. So the idea that some people are motivated and others aren't is a myth. The truth is that everyone is motivated. They may not be motivated by the same things that motivate you or by what you think should motivate them. However, all breathing humans are most definitely motivated.

According to Urban Meyer, head coach of the University of Florida's national championship football team, "The old adage about 'treating everybody the same' [is something with which] I cannot disagree more. You have to get to know someone before you can understand how to coach them, how to treat them, how to get the most out of them."[9] ADT executive Georgia Eddleman agrees: "You've got to make the effort to know your people and to understand what motivates them. Each person does what they do for their own reasons; they don't do things for your reasons. You really have to understand what is motivating people so that you can show them how the things you want them to do are in their best interest."

For example, sometimes the very best people don't want any attention, says Chuck Blumenkamp. "They'll say, 'Please, I love my job, this company, my customers. Thank you for recognizing me—but I really don't want to stand up in front of people. Please don't make me.' So what do you do? You tell people that Sharon was number one again for the fifth year in a row. But don't make her stand up. In fact, if she doesn't want to come to the ceremony, that's okay. With those kinds of things, you've got to know your people well enough that they're comfortable telling you if they're uncomfortable."

Opportunity in a Crisis

In tough times, you need more than ever the loyalty and discretionary effort of your people. To get it, you've got to exercise your greatest source of power and change the way they feel. This means helping them channel their anxiety and uncertainty into something they can believe in and giving them something meaningful to do. Pull it off, and two good things can happen. In the short term, you get the heightened performance you need. In the long term, your organization emerges from the crisis with an even stronger culture.

Case in point: Severe acute respiratory syndrome—more widely known as SARS—hit Southeast Asia in 2003, infecting over 8,000 people and killing nearly 800. Very quickly, 80 percent of business travel and tourism to Vietnam evaporated.

Our colleague Binh Nguyen was working at the time at the Duxton Hotel in Ho Chi Minh City. His boss, the hotel manager, faced some tough choices and spent a few days agonizing over what to do. Finally, he brought all his employees together in the hotel's grand ballroom. "You all know about SARS and what it has done to our business," he said. "And you've seen other hotels in the city cutting jobs by 40 percent." Everyone nodded, prepared for the worst. Then he said, "I also understand that you still have your family to feed. I know what will happen if you don't have a job. So I have an idea." The manager then explained two options: The hotel could cut jobs by 40 percent, or everyone could take a 40 percent pay cut but no one would lose their job.

He allowed his employees to ask questions and discuss the options. Then he conducted a vote by secret ballot. Ninety-two percent of employees elected to reduce salaries so that everyone could stay.

As one employee recalls, "From that day forward, things changed. Employees came to see each other as brothers and sisters. Before, there was a lot of fighting going on between different departments. But after the vote, everyone recognized that their fellow employees were protecting them and helping them keep their jobs."

That led to more than just camaraderie, however; it produced a sense of ownership and investment. Employees who previously had just "punched the clock" for the first time started coming up with ideas for how to cut costs. For example, because occupancy was only 20 to 30 percent, one staff member came up with the idea to close down the top floors. They turned off all the lights, shut off the water, and assigned just one person to upkeep for those floors. They also stopped printing out reports for managers, and used e-mail and other means instead. All together, they saved a billion Vietnamese dong on electricity, water, paper, and other small things. As one employee recalls, "The more we worked together, the more money we saved, and the more our morale grew."

And then something even better happened. When the World Health Organization declared Vietnam SARS-free, tourism started picking up again. Guests poured in, and all of a sudden, every hotel in Ho Chi Minh City was up to full occupancy. For weeks, other hotels didn't have enough staff to meet guest demands and had to turn people away because they couldn't accommodate them. But at the Duxton, they had a full staff and could meet all their guests' needs. Other hotels had to go find new employees and then train them, which took at least three months before they were fully up and running again.

And the best part? When those other hotels came to Duxton employees offering them more money to go work elsewhere, not a single Duxton employee left. "Because we had trust," one of them explained to us. "We knew that if SARS or another crisis struck again, the other hotels would throw us into the streets. But we believed that even if we got paid a little less, we'd be safe at the Duxton. So we stayed. We all stayed."

CHAPTER 8

WIELD YOUR BIGGEST STICK: THE POWER TO TAKE THINGS AWAY

We just explained why your greatest source of power is your ability to change how people feel. We noted that one of the ways to use this power is to harness human-kind's hardwired aversion to loss—which makes us much more sensitive to losses than to equivalent gains. In short, one of the most effective ways to drive accountability is to make sure that people who aren't doing what's needed lose something that they value.

In this chapter we'll expand on this concept, describing some proven techniques for leveraging loss aversion to make bad behavior more costly. We think it's worth noting that with only one exception, these techniques don't involve money, yet they all work.

Team Trust

- *Bad behavior*—Failure to pull one's own weight, letting down the team
- *Cost of bad behavior*—Loss of teammates' confidence

There are a lot of benefits to building a strong team. One of the most underappreciated is the sense of collective accountability you'll find in teams that are highly cohesive. According to the players of football powerhouse University of Florida, Coach Urban Meyer "preaches family a lot. Our teammates are our brothers. You never want to let family down. The feeling of letting a teammate down is so much worse than letting the coach down—because the coach is still going to coach you. If you let your teammate down, there's no telling if he can trust you on the field again or not."[1]

In a different context, Mike Sanchez, CEO of CycleLife USA, applies the same principle with his team. He says: "You can use something as simple as a weekly status meeting to create positive peer influence. It's really a way to make people accountable." Sanchez's idea is to use the social bonds between people to positively influence them to stick to their word. "You said you were going to do the signs for our bike valet service for the Nationals' games. How did that go?" Nobody wants to tell their teammates, who are following through on their own commitments, "Um, yeah, I didn't do that."

Soft Shaming

- *Bad behavior*—Failure to perform or feigning clarity
- *Cost of bad behavior*—Loss of face; loss of anonymous noncompliance

We call these techniques *soft shaming* because they involve only asking questions and reporting facts; they don't involve labeling anyone a bad person or subjecting that person to public humiliation. But they nonetheless rely on the motivating power of people not wanting to "look bad" to others (e.g., peers, their boss, etc.).

Here's an example: Earlier, we talked about using commander's intent (CI) as a way to align an organization around strategy. One of the ways to push the message to everyone in the organization is via a structured cascade, where the senior leader meets with his or her directs, they meet with their directs, and so forth until everyone in the organization has met with his or her immediate leader and peers to talk about the strategy, ask questions about it, and decide how they can take action to support it.

Often, when we recommend a structured cascade to a new client, they'll say: "Sounds great. But we've tried cascades before. They don't work here. The message tends to peter out after it has reached only 20 percent of the organization. Too many managers fail to pass along the message, and it stalls out." To which our response is: "Cascades aren't the problem; accountability is. We need to make your managers' noncompliance more costly."

How do we do that? We ask every manager to provide feedback after they've cascaded the message to their team. Simple questions: *How did the conversation go? What questions were you asked that you need help answering? And what is your team planning to do to act on the message?*

The feedback process generates useful data—but it also makes it possible to identify who has complied and who hasn't. Those who cascade the message and provide feedback by the deadline get a "carrot" message from the senior leader (e.g., "Thanks for the feedback"). Those who don't get a "stick" (e.g., "We've received feedback from most of your peers, but we're still waiting for yours"). We also recommend updating and sending out each day a graph showing compliance rates by department, ranked from highest to lowest. By taking these simple steps to create social consequences, compliance for cascading messages shoots from 20 to 98 to 100 percent in every organization in which we've ever tried it.

Of course, the use of this type of social consequence isn't limited to cascades. Our colleague Robin Abramson works with a leader who, in a town hall, said, "We have these strategic priorities, and I want to know what your group is doing to meet them. I'm serious. So serious that if your last name ends in P, R, D, Q, or S, send me an e-mail telling me what your group is doing." As it turns out, only one person did it. So the leader actually forwarded that e-mail to everyone and said, "I asked you to send me this, and only one person did. It's great what he's doing with his team, and now

I expect to hear from the rest of you." It was a huge carrot for the individual who sent the e-mail, and it was a little, but powerful stick for those who didn't. "Using social pressure like this is hugely motivating for people," Robin says.

You also can leverage "loss of face aversion" in one-on-one settings. Nguyen Toan, the PetroVietnam executive whom we introduced earlier, leads teams that build oil platforms and other technical installations. It's dangerous work. Because of this, "people need to ask questions when they don't understand," he says. "But when they don't understand, they're often embarrassed. So my goal is to make it more embarrassing to *pretend* to know the answers than to ask questions when you're not sure."

How does he do this? "When someone says, 'Yes, sir,' I now ask, 'What does "Yes, sir" mean?' I ask them to tell me again what they understand. When I first started doing this, most people could clearly repeat back to me my expectations only about 50 to 60 percent of the time. So then I would explain it again. Then I'd watch them. If they were doing it right, I wouldn't have to follow them any more."

Competition

- *Bad behavior*—Lackluster effort
- *Cost of bad behavior*—Loss of pride or "bragging rights"

Competitions and friendly wagers are another way to motivate discretionary effort. People want to win . . . and they hate to lose. "We use the old idea from *Built to Last*," says Vanguard Chairman Jack Brennan. "We set BHAGs (Big Hairy Audacious Goals). And we have BHAG bets with the crew members every year, where what's at stake might be two days off. We focus the bets on things that really matter—where we really should be focusing attention— because the bets do create energy and attention."

Another way to leverage loss aversion through competition is the approach we use when we facilitate sessions for clients who say they want to improve their performance. What we found years ago is that if we asked a team at an offsite to collectively identify some things they don't do well, they might feel a little defensive, and it might take us an entire afternoon to coax from them a couple of decent ideas and a "next action" or two. Not the honesty and earnest engagement we were looking for.

The solution, we found, is to divide the participants into two or more "consulting teams"; ask each consulting team to generate a team name, mascot, and slogan (so they feel a real sense of identification); and then give them a couple of hours to analyze the overall group's opportunities for improvement and generate specific recommendations. We then ask them to present their ideas in head-to-head competition with the other consulting team(s). Because it's a competition, and bragging rights are at stake, they inevitably work through lunch and the scheduled breaks, engage in highly self-critical analysis, and generate very specific recommendations for improvement. They end up providing themselves with the core elements of a rich and robust improvement plan. The pursuit of honor in competition overrides the instinctive defensiveness and laziness that made our previous approach ineffective. Under the new, competition-driven approach, participants often tell us they've never before worked so hard in a team offsite. And occasionally, after the session, they'll suggest the possibility that we manipulated their emotions, to which we concede, "Yes, and benevolently so."

Confrontation Therapy

- *Bad behavior*—Making unrealistic commitments; procrastination; failure to follow through on good intentions
- *Cost of bad behavior*—Loss of illusion about self-defeating behavior

Some time ago we asked Alex Gwozda, our wunderkind intern, if he would serve as project manager on a very important, high-stakes project. Alex had no formal training as a project manager. And he knew that many of the people working on the project, who happened to be in different locations across the United States, had a track record of overcommitting (though driven only by good intentions). There were, perhaps, some serial procrastinators in the mix as well.

Alex agreed to take on the role, provided that we gave him license to have tough conversations with the people whose activity he was tracking. *Confrontation therapy*, we called it. The approach has its roots in the work of the influential psychologist Albert Ellis. Ellis believed that behaviors such as procrastination, avoidance, and overcommitment result from irrational thinking and self-defeating behavior. The fix is a process in which the therapist actively helps the client to identify his or her irrational and self-defeating beliefs and behaviors, forcefully and actively questions and confronts them, and replaces them with beliefs and behaviors that are more rational and helpful.[2]

Here's how it played out: The first set of project deadlines came and went, and only a couple of people actually hit their marks. Some got their deliverables to Alex the next day. A few of them made convincing efforts to explain their tardiness.

Alex could have let them off the hook and hoped for better next time, like many of the formally trained project managers we've seen in organizations. Instead, he sent out some e-mails. They went something like this:

Hi Mary,

Thanks for doing your piece this morning.

It was a day late, however. I wanted to give you the opportunity to let me know what you're going to do to prevent being late on your upcoming deadlines. What do you plan to change about your process to make sure you're happily on time?

A response within 1 to 3 hours would work best, when you have a minute to reflect.

Alex

When Alex didn't get responses, he'd call cell phones. That's when the magic happened. Here's the e-mail that Mary sent, unprompted, to the whole team the next day:

I said to Alex, "So what do I need to do to be accountable?" After a lengthy and pregnant pause, he said softly: "Well, I thought that might be something you would reflect on." Zen-therapist bastard . . . he had a point!

After deciding I had no reason to be mad at him, I admitted the root cause to be a procrastination tendency, not the cold I'd blamed. I committed to buy a book called, The Now Habit: A Strategic Program for Overcoming Procrastination and Enjoying Guilt-Free Play, *to help me address my deeper illness.*

Thanks Alex. I've ordered the book.

Best . . .

Mary"

Soon after, Mary began updating the project calendar with her milestones, which she had professed she hated doing, and two weeks later she mentioned to Alex, surprised, that it really wasn't that bad anymore.

"My aim wasn't to be a jerk; I wanted to help people improve their ability to perform on the project," Alex said. "I tried to remember that even when I sensed they didn't want to talk to me. Uncertainty, disappointment, anger, resentment, and thinly veiled disgust—all these emotions can appear when people are forced to acknowledge and confront their well-disguised bad habits that are sabotaging their efforts."

The conclusion of this experiment? Confrontation therapy makes well-intentioned overcommitters and procrastinators uncomfortable, but it works because it strips them of their illusions that support their self-defeating behavior.

Alex adds: "Despite many awkward moments and some grumbling, *every single person on the team thanked me at least once for treating them this way.* It became clear from what I was hearing that I was not just helping to complete the project . . . but also helping the people on it become better performers themselves. All this from an intern/neophyte project manager. To have an influence in this kind of progress is truly rewarding—doubly so if you don't mind watching people squirm to get there!"

Alex the Intern's Four Recommendations for Project Managers

1. *Ask, exactly what happened?* Be sure to really listen to their reasons and excuses and situations and woes.

Whether justified or not, it's important that people feel that you understand where they're coming from. However they are going to resolve their situation, it will only happen if it makes sense from their perspective. So try to truly understand them.

2. *Ask, how will you prevent this in the future?*

3. *Ask, don't tell.* Do not try to tell people how *they* are going to prevent *their* tardiness in the future! This tramples their sense of personal responsibility and can breed permanent resentment. Instead, *ask* them what they're going to do differently to make sure it doesn't happen again. You might be surprised at what they come up with.

4. *Ask them to choose one specific work-related habit that they will change.* They may need your help to see things more clearly, but you should resist making suggestions unless they're absolutely floundering. Holding them to their own ideas is much more effective. Further, they themselves choose what their extra effort will be, so they can't blame you for giving them a solution that doesn't work.

Commitment Contracts

- *Bad behavior*—Failure to follow through on commitments and good intentions
- *Cost of bad behavior*—Loss of money (possibly to a cause or person to whom you emphatically do not wish to lose it)

Dean Karlan and Ian Ayres are professors at Yale and they've created a company called *stickK.com* (where Jeff now moonlights as a senior advisor). Based on Dean and Ian's research and personal experience, stickK's Web site allows people to set up commitment contracts. Commitment contracts help people to follow through on their good intentions by increasing the cost of failure. The process is simple: You make a commitment, you put some money at stake, select a referee to hold you accountable, and then work toward your goal. If you follow through on your commitment (and your referee vouches that you have), you get your money back. If not, you forfeit it.

The seeds of stickK were sown when Dean was an economics graduate student at MIT. Dean realized that he'd gotten heavier than he'd ever been before, and his friend had the same problem. They made an agreement, each staking a big chunk of his annual income, that they would lose nearly 40 pounds by a particular deadline. By raising the cost of failure and agreeing that they would referee for each other and wouldn't let each other off the hook, both found the motivation to hit their goals.

While you don't have to use stickK.com to create a commitment contract, the site simplifies the process, making it easy to enter the goal, set the stakes, and invite a referee. (You also can use tools at the site to let your friends know about the commitment you've made, further increasing the cost of failure. Blow it, and you lose face, not just money.)

What happens to the money forfeited by the weak-willed souls who fail to follow through on their contracts? It goes to charity. "But not a charity you choose," says stickK's CEO Jordan Goldberg, "because that would make the loss less painful; you could rationalize you were doing a good thing." Indeed, one of the coolest things about stickK is that they encourage you to select an *anticharity* to receive your money if you fail to fulfill the terms of your contract.

What's an anticharity? It's an organization that supports a cause or a position contrary to your own. The prospect of losing your money to a cause you have a strong aversion to magnifies the power of loss aversion. For example, if you are pro-life, think about how much it will pain you to forfeit your money to the National Abortion Rights Action League. If you favor gun control, think about how much it will pain you to forfeit your money to the National Rifle Association. This is the simple brilliance of stickK—you choose the consequence that is going to make failure hurt a lot more than doing whatever it takes to succeed.

There are a variety of practical uses for stickK and commitment contracts for leaders who are working to increase accountability.

Does your team make commitments and then back away from them over time? Chronically miss the targets they set for themselves? Insist they are going to do one thing but then find excuses when they can't? Try this: The next time your team assures you that they are going to follow through on something and you have your doubts, create a commitment contract. Have each individual team member pick an anticharity or choose a collective anticharity such as a rival team or organization to which it will hurt to forfeit the stakes of the contract.

Do you ever bring in an expensive trainer or speaker to equip your team with some new leadership skills and behaviors? Everybody walks away jazzed up and committed to putting what he or she has learned into action. But then they get back to the day-to-day grind and never get around to changing their habits? Your return on investment is zilch. You can change that by having your people create commitment contracts at the end of the session. This is what we recommend every time we're asked to speak about *leadership without excuses*.

Speaking of shameless plugs, have you ever read a leadership book and committed to putting some of its coaching points into action—but then failed to do so? As it relates to applying the principles from *this* book, we're going to take away your excuses. In the book's conclusion, we'll point you to a custom version of the stickK.com Web site where you can make contracts to follow through on your good intentions to create accountability and high performance— instead of just talking about it.

Something That Doesn't Work

In the best-seller *Freakonomics,*[3] the authors describe what happened when a day care center wanted to cut down on the frequency with which parents were late to pick up their children. To solve the problem, the center instituted a $3 fine for each late pickup. To the day care center's chagrin, tardiness more than doubled! The problem? "For just a few dollars each day, parents could buy off [the] guilt" they felt for arriving late.

In our experience, the same principle applies to the practice used by some leaders of putting a jar on the table in team meetings and fining participants $5 each time they curse or use their iPhones or BlackBerries while others are speaking. It doesn't eliminate the bad behavior; it often increases it. The fine isn't large enough to create a real disincentive, and those who pay it no longer feel any guilt about doing something they shouldn't. It's paying (a small price) for indulgences.

CHAPTER 9

WHEN YOU HAVE NO AUTHORITY, USE INCREASED CONFIDENCE AND REDUCED ANXIETY AS YOUR CONSEQUENCE CURRENCY

If anyone deserves to make excuses, it's got to be the folks who lead corporate functions (information technology, finance, etc.) and the corporate-based project teams responsible for major business initiatives (including ERPs and EMRs—if you don't know, *don't* ask). Managing their own reports is the easy part of the job. To deliver the results on which they've staked their livelihoods and reputations, these masochists also must persuade their "clients"—namely, people outside headquarters who generate actual revenue for the company—to implement new, often unproven ways of doing things. In exchange for this privilege, these clients typically also must subsidize millions of dollars in project costs and consulting fees. What's not to love?

It's true: Getting people to do stuff when you have no positional authority over them is enormously challenging.

When we talk to corporate function and business initiative leaders about creating the conditions of accountability for their stakeholders, they often respond incredulously, "Your model doesn't apply to our internal clients. We can't fire them, promote them, or give them bonuses. In short, we can't create consequences for these people." To which our response is, respectively, "True. True. True. And nothing could be further from the truth."

You're already creating consequences for these people, and therein lies the problem.

Increasing Confidence and Reducing Anxiety

We said it earlier, and we'll say it again: The measure of any consequence is the extent to which it influences the way the recipient *feels*.

How do these clients and stakeholders want to feel? On behalf of the leaders we work with, we've surveyed and interviewed thousands of internal clients and stakeholders. And while the specific findings vary from company to company and industry to industry, there is a common thread in every single study of this type we have ever conducted. They all want to feel more confident—confident, for example, that what they're investing in is going to help them make their numbers and deliver the results on which they've staked *their* resources and reputations. And they want to feel less anxiety—about the unexpected, about the reliability of the systems and processes on which they count, about losing autonomy to people who don't understand their needs, and about looking like idiots. This is a very powerful finding. It means that if you find a way to increase your internal clients' and stakeholders' confidence and reduce their anxiety, they will give you anything you want. Anything.

Your problem is: Even before you darken their doorway, the function or initiative you represent is probably doing the opposite. To understand why you may not be increasing confidence and reducing anxiety, put yourself in their shoes.

Example: You're a top physician, widely respected by your peers, learning that the organization plans to replace your paper charts with electronic medical records. This means that you're going to have to change the way you've practiced medicine for 20 years and, um, learn to type. Oh, and try to forget what you've heard at medical conferences—that the system your hospital is implementing is a bit buggy because the vendor frequently updates the software. *Where's your confidence? How's your anxiety?*

Another example: You've worked hard and risen to the top tier of management in your region. You're generally well liked, in part because you always find a way to deliver results. In a slumping economy, though, there's more pressure than ever to do more with less. So you're pushing yourself and your people harder than ever. At the same time, corporate has sent word that you're supposed to start using some new tools, templates, and processes for doing things. But don't worry because some well-known companies—albeit in completely different industries—have done the same thing, and everyone knows how admired and successful they are. *Where's your confidence? How's your anxiety?*

If you're a leader in a corporate function or business initiative and that's the kind of challenge you're up against, how do you create the conditions of accountability for the clients and stakeholders out in the business that you need to influence and engage? You have to make choices that create for them more than enough confidence and reduce for them more than enough anxiety to erase the deficits you started from. Here are six ways to help make that happen.

Confidence Comes from Relationships

In the United States, there's an interesting political phenomenon. Going back decades, more than half of Americans have told pollsters they have an unfavorable opinion of Congress. But come election time, Americans typically reelect more than 90 percent of congressional incumbents. How do you explain this contradiction? Simple. Our capacity to develop affection for institutions (like Congress) is never as great as our capacity to develop affection for specific people ("my own representative"). The same principle applies inside organizations. Everybody hates information technology (almost as much as they hate human resources). But if you make the right choices, they may come to appreciate and value *you*.

Jose-Luis Bretones-Lopez, whom you met in Chapter 2, is a director for a large, well-known multinational company. He learned this lesson in the process of driving the implementation of new planning and project management tools in the company's operations throughout the company's Asia Pacific and Middle East regions. When he headed abroad on his first trip there, he thought: "Even though I am new to the company and nobody knows me, I do have one thing in my favor: I'm an expert from corporate. They'll be happy to see me because I am bringing a new perspective, great ideas, and solutions to their problems."

"That was a bit naive," he laughs. "They thought, 'He's going to come in, stay for a day, go to a couple of meetings, and assume he understands the situation here. Then he will criticize most of what we are doing locally; he'll hop back on the plane and expect we're going to move in a new direction.'"

He learned soon enough that he needed to earn their trust before he could make any progress. "After my initial failures, I pulled back on talking about project management," he says. Instead, he extended his trips and spent more time in the field asking a lot of questions so that he could understand the situation. He was openly humble about his ignorance regarding the local nuances.

He also made an effort to learn about his stakeholders' families, hobbies, and interests. "Like most of them, I started my career in a small field office, a little factory in Spain close to my parent's house," Jose-Luis says. "So I looked for opportunities to talk about my family and my background. Most of all, I dedicated time to prove I truly cared to understand. After we built personal relationships, we really started working together effectively."

Something that's worked wonders for many of the leaders we coach is a simple but mindful approach to building and managing their stakeholder relationships. We start by asking questions:

- First: "To produce the results to which you've committed, who are the stakeholders (people over whom you have no positional authority) you need to effectively influence and engage over the next six months?" We encourage the leader to pare down the list to 12 people, at least to start; few people can effectively focus on cultivating more than a dozen relationships.
- Next, we ask for each key stakeholder: "If you flawlessly build and nurture this relationship, what will be true six months from now?" For example, what will this stakeholder have done or be doing? What will he or she believe about you? What kind of relationship will you have?
- After the leader has thought about and articulated his or her goals for each relationship, we help the leader to identify, for each key stakeholder, the next single action he or she will take to move toward the desired

outcome. Building trust is a gradual process and almost always involves multiple steps. But it's also an iterative process, which is why we focus on identifying only the next action (instead of mapping out the next six actions for any particular relationship, which is usually a waste of time).

- Next, we set up a plan to talk with the leader every two weeks or so to review progress and to identify the next round of actions for each key stakeholder relationship. And the process continues for as long as necessary.

If you want to set up a system like this for yourself but don't have access to a coach, you can enroll a colleague to be your relationship management "whip." To play this role effectively, the whip must

- Be vigilant—and obnoxious, if necessary—about scheduling time with you every couple of weeks
- Be willing to offer you a dispassionate, outside perspective on your key stakeholder relationships and strategies for developing them
- Give you significant grief when you commit to next actions but fail to follow through on them

Here's an example of a stakeholder management action plan used by one of our clients based on the approach described:

Stakeholder	Targeted Outcomes (Actions, Attitudes, Relationship Rules, etc.)	Next Actions for 6/1 to 6/15
Ralph	He respects me to the degree to which I can go to him with a suggestion and not have to sell it to him as his own. He perceives alignment.	This week: Provide him status and forecast for June/July visit (anything we need to talk about before then?).
Dominick	He takes my advice on the value his organization could have.	Ask him to dinner or lunch. Ask him to articulate the barriers to getting to where we have already agreed is an ideal destination.
Kelsey	He doesn't give me the "nod." He comes to me more.	Continue *not* going to his meetings. Ask him to validate my strategy for managing one of my other stakeholder relationships.
Alexa	I better understand her drivers and leverage points.	This week: Talk to Shawn about going there to meet her. Ask for advice on how to most effectively engage her.
Ron	I have improved visibility with him.	Talk to Jim L about setting up a monthly status discussion with Ron (and Jim L).
Randy	He thinks of me as more of a peer; I don't have to keep proving myself to him.	Put "on the table" the fact that he's the only person who sees a dotted-line relationship, but that, regardless, you want to stay in synch.

Speak Their Language

Of course, you want to show your stakeholders that you know stuff. You want them to appreciate your expertise. So you liberally sprinkle into your conversations the jargon associated with your craft. And in your e-mail signature you add after your name any designation you've earned (e.g., black belt, ITIL, etc.). Will this accomplish just what we advised you to do—enhance confidence and reduce anxiety?

Sorry, but no. Millennia ago, humans developed the ability to quickly read subtle cues to sort everyone we encounter as either "in tribe" or "out of tribe." If you're a caveman and you know that everyone around is a fellow tribesperson, you can let down your guard and devote your energy to hunting, gathering, or finding a mate. But when members of other tribes are in your midst, you wisely stay wary. The "quick scan and sort" is a survival mechanism.

We know lots of people who, in their well-intentioned but misguided effort to share the gospel of lean Six Sigma or some other creed, use specialized language. They present themselves in such a way that they would do just as well to shout, "I am from a *different* tribe. And I don't mean from over the hill. I'm talking way *distant* tribe here. And the longer I stay, the more likely it is that *I am going to seriously mess with your way of life.*"

Words matter. As Richard Conniff wrote, "Groups . . . frequently develop their own . . . language. It's often a practical tool full of technical terms relevant to the problem at hand. But it also serves as a means of identifying members and folding them into the group's embrace while freezing out intruders. The members of the in-group share certain viewpoints, values, language, and other markers. People who don't dress or talk the 'right' way can become almost invisible. *It becomes easier to inflict pain on them without guilt"* (emphasis ours).[1]

A few years ago we worked with a leader of an insurance giant, whose chief executive officer (CEO) had recruited him to bring process and systems thinking to an important part of the organization that desperately needed it. One of his first steps was to make the rounds to introduce himself and forecast expectations about what he was planning to do. Knowing that more than a few management fads and programs had already come and gone in the organization's recent history, he chose his language carefully and focused on his intentions to help people in the organization "find smarter ways to make decisions and better ways to get things done." After one particular meet-and-greet, an employee approached him and said, "Hey, I'm new to the organization, too. I'm guessing you have a Six Sigma background." To which the new leader replied, "Yes, I'm a master black belt. But if you tell anyone I'm going to kill you." Hyperbole, sure. But he understood what was at stake. When we talked about it later, he observed, "Why should we expect any support if we can't explain to the business in the simple, conversational language they already use why we would be doing this?"

This is another of the important lessons that Jose-Luis learned from his experience in Asia. "At first, I thought I should create a brand around what I was trying to do. So I started calling it PPM—program and project management," he says. "I wanted to see if I could get people to start talking about PPM, bringing it up in planning meetings and management meetings. My goal was to create the PPM brand, push it through the ranks, and spread the word."

After some success in building real relationships with his stakeholders, he found that they were genuinely interested in the underlying concepts he was promoting. "But," he says, "I also found that when I'd throw out a new concept or a definition like PPM, instead of just absorbing it, they were stuck on trying to translate it into words they were already familiar with."

So he stopped trying to get them to adopt *his* language. "They were already familiar with the concept of business planning, as they did it at the country level at least once a year. And they knew their business, of course, and understood well the gaps and the opportunities. They just didn't see program and project management as an improvement," Jose-Luis says. "Once I 'got it,' I adopted their language, which made it much easier to talk about gaps, opportunities, and solutions. And then they adopted a more disciplined approach to the overall business planning process. So it worked. That they go around talking about it in my language was not a requirement for declaring the work a success."

And so Jose-Luis walked away with a good reputation as a trusted advisor. He became known as someone who could help to improve business—that's something everyone can appreciate—as opposed to being merely someone who has expertise in something nobody thinks they need.

Always With, Never To

When she's at her day job, Susan Olofson helps different groups (including labor/management and information technology (IT)/the rest of the business) bridge their differences to get things done. When she's not at work, she does pretty much the same thing. This is so because she uses her vacation time to facilitate educational projects in East Africa on behalf of the Asante Africa Foundation.

She recently partnered with a Polish team to build a school in a remote Maasai village. There was tension—a result of different perspectives and experience—between the Poles and the Maasai even before construction started.

There is no Maasai word for stranger—they welcome all newcomers as visitors with open hearts and homes. "So the conventions of business we take for granted—including the need to clarify details and challenge ideas with which you don't agree—are literally foreign there," Susan says.

On the other hand, "the Poles incorrectly assumed that their experiences with other East African tribes were transferable to the Maasai. They operated as if their education and experience made them the natural leaders in the situation rather than seeing the true client relationship they needed to nurture with the village chief," Susan says. "They failed to fully appreciate the intelligence and wisdom of the culture in which they were working. And so their good intentions missed the mark. Without knowing it, they were disrupting the Maasai way of life."

During one meeting in a thatched-roof hut, the chief's patience was wearing thin as he listened to the details of an operating agreement the Poles wanted him to sign on the spot. As his agitation grew, the Polish project leader turned to Susan with a smile and said, "I think the chief doesn't understand." As he rose, Susan could see that the chief, a trained warrior who carries hand weapons for protection from lions and such, had lost his patience with the other tribe.

Susan intervened, saying, "Wait, Chief, is it that you don't understand, or that you don't agree?"

"I don't agree," he said, and he voiced his objections to the conditions presented. This marked a shift in their relationship moving forward, establishing his role as the ultimate decision maker. Over the following weeks, Susan continued to facilitate meetings and coach the Maasai leaders on how Westerners operate in business. And from then on, they were able to move the project along much more smoothly.

"The traps here were the assumption of power, presenting information in ways the receiver can't relate to or process, and mistaking tolerance and hospitality for acceptance of business ideas," Susan says. "Whether you're in a conference room or a Maasai hut, those are the ingredients of doing things *to* rather than *with* or *for* your stakeholders."

If you want to increase your stakeholders' confidence and reduce their anxiety (as opposed to the inverse), it's not enough to speak your stakeholders' language. You've got to put them front and center as your reason to exist. No one likes solutions imposed from the outside.

Dave Watson, CIO/CTO at MedeFinance, says, "A lot of people think I do technology. But what I actually do is use technology to enable change." Some of his colleagues used to look at him like he was from Mars when he'd say, "There are no 'IT initiatives,' just business initiatives with IT components." Dave believes that "Everything we do is for the business. Otherwise, we better not do it."

One of the things that he's learned is that you should never start an initiative without the right sponsorship. If you're going to start something, it must be started well, which means at the top. (Maybe this sounds obvious, but you'd be surprised how many senior leaders distance themselves from large projects—probably because they know how few of them succeed.) If it's a big corporate transformation, the CEO is the only acceptable sponsor. Yet too many initiatives proceed without the right sponsorship.

"But I was trying to do the right thing for the company," people will say. To which Dave responds: "Yes, and it will be 'the right thing to do' that will fail miserably. Because we're doing it *to* them, instead of doing it *with* them." He adds: "In some states, you can go to prison for that."

Are there other applications of the "*with*, not *to*" principle? "Our stakeholders want to be educated, not lectured," says Kaiser Permanente Chief Procurements Officer Dean Edwards. "There's no point in acting incredulous when you learn that some practice that was taken for granted in your last organization seems foreign in the new one. When our stakeholders are 'behind the times,' it is more likely a poor reflection on us than it is on them." Working from that perspective, he and his team try to show stakeholders what's possible and how to turn intention into action. For example, he says, "We've done a lot of work with our internal clients to educate them on how to more effectively deal with vendors—by raising expectations and creating the conditions of accountability."

Take the Long View

Jose-Luis learned another great lesson while assigned to his company's Asia-Pacific region: "I came to see the power of giving away my best ideas to the people who had the credibility to carry them," he says.

Kenneth, the general manager in Singapore, was delivering some very impressive results. One day Jose-Luis realized that Kenneth could drive change better than he could. "Obviously, the price I'd pay is that my name wouldn't be associated with Singapore's progress or results," Jose-Luis said. But, he thought, "You know what? I'm going to teach this guy everything I know, let him run with whatever works for him, and take myself out of the picture entirely." He knew that when things were over, Kenneth might not even remember his name. But he also knew that even if that happened, he could "point to Singapore and the new things they were doing as a model of success."

It worked and got results. "The credit rightfully belongs to him and his team," Jose-Luis says modestly. "But I actually ended up with some credit, too."

The best part, he says, was the win-win: "I equipped him with new tools and insights about program and project management that were useful to him. And at the same time I learned a lot from Kenneth about the connections and the leverage points in the region and some of their day-to-day challenges that I had never fully understood. Understanding those connection points helped me tremendously later in my work with other countries."

Giving away his best ideas is something Jose-Luis has done many times since. "Sometimes I get credit, and sometimes I don't. And sometimes it comes later, when you get a call from somebody who has just met Kenneth and heard about what we did in Singapore and wants to do the same thing." He adds: "As long as the business improves, that's what matters. You may not get any credit 70 percent of the time, but if you believe in what you're doing, 30 percent is plenty to keep you going."

Dean Edwards of Kaiser Permanente tells a similar story. When he was working in procurement for a large drug maker, the brand team for a particular product came to him and said they wanted to fire their ad agency. "They're no good. Their stuff is crap," they said. The brand team wanted to bring in a particular big-name agency. Dean looked into it and came back to them and said, "The new agency will cost at least two or three times what you're paying now. You've been underpaying your existing firm for five years, and so they're not putting the right people on the account. Why don't we find out what it would take to get the incumbent to put the right people on the account? Give them six months to turn it around and see what happens." Long story short, they ended up paying the incumbent agency 50 percent more—but that's much less than they would have spent with the big-name agency. And more important, because they started getting what they needed, they were able to increase revenue by $100 million. "We made them look like geniuses," Dean says. "Did *we* get credit? Of course not."

"But," he adds, "I didn't walk away empty-handed. The experience equipped me with a story I can share with our internal clients to challenge conventional thinking about procurement—and illustrate what it means to approach procurement strategically. It's not just about cost savings, it's about solving problems—and in most cases, making them look good."

In a Crisis, Show You Care

When something goes wrong, we too often see corporate functions do things that zap confidence and exacerbate anxiety among their internal clients and stakeholders.

Fingerpointing. It almost never works to shift the blame to another corporate function or department within your own function. No one out in the field cares about your organization chart and the lines between your functional silos. To them, you're all from that corporate tribe who can't get its act together.

Silence. When mission-critical systems fail, IT focuses its attention on solving the problem. And too often it operates from the working assumption that "when we know something, we'll share it." As crisis management expert Helio Fred Garcia points out, though, whether your stakeholders are external customers or internal clients, silence kills reputations. His advice? If you are the first to define the problem, what's behind it, and the response, you'll be okay. But if your critics out in the business or elsewhere define the crisis, what's behind it, and what needs to happen, you're likely to suffer. "The single biggest predictor of harm in a crisis," Fred says, "is the perception that leaders just don't care. People forgive organizations all the time, even when very bad things happen. But they can't forgive you—won't forgive you—if they perceive indifference. And the longer the indifference lasts, the harder it is to get back to neutral." For more on this topic, see Fred's sidebar below.

In a Crisis? Avoid Self-Inflicted Harm

By Helio Fred Garcia, President, Logos Consulting

In a crisis, the worst harm done is self-inflicted. It is the result of ignoring problems, denying their severity, lying about them, or otherwise failing to confront the bad things that leaders pretend not to know.

We all remember the delay in marshaling government resources to help the victims of the New Orleans hurricane and flood in August 2005. President George W. Bush was viewed as having risen to the occasion after the 9/11 attacks on the World Trade Center and the Pentagon, but in the days immediately after Katrina, he was criticized for seeming disengaged, uninformed, and unconcerned about the plight of New Orleans citizens.

After three days, FEMA Chief Michael Brown appeared on each of the network news programs and admitted that the government had been unaware of thousands of people stranded in the New Orleans Convention Center for several days without food and water, despite the fact that it had been widely reported by those very same television news programs for days. He had to be told about the situation in the interview. He flailed around, looking helpless. Brown immediately became the butt of late-night comedians' jokes. But two days later, the president, invoking the FEMA chief's nickname, told him on television, "Brownie, you're doing a heck of a job."

Two weeks passed as the federal response was just getting into full swing. *Time* magazine's Web site published a cartoon of a man standing waist deep in water, holding a sign that implored, "Leadership Please."[2] The next day, Brown resigned. That week President Bush's approval ratings fell to then-record lows and continued to fall.[3] Six months after Katrina hit, President Bush's approval rating dropped to the low 30s and never recovered. That's a warning to leaders. These are the consequences of avoiding the unpleasant and appearing indifferent.

When something bad happens that my clients would prefer to ignore or deny, I tell them to ask themselves four questions:

1. Will those who matter to us expect us to do or say something now?
2. Will silence be seen as indifference to the harm the crisis is causing?
3. Are others speaking about us, shaping the perception about us among those who matter to us? Will they soon?
4. If we wait, will we lose the ability to determine the outcome?

If the answer to any one of these questions is "Yes," my advice is: Overcome the inertia, fear, and inattention and respond now!

Don't Kill Yourself for a –1

One of our colleagues, Dr. John Daly of the University of Texas, has a great metaphor for explaining what social scientists call *expectancy violation theory*. He says that when an experience matches our expectations, it tends to register as a zero in our long-term memory. In other words, we don't remember it. This explains why, even if you're happily married, you can't remember what your spouse gave you for your birthday three years ago. Whatever it was, it fell within the range of expected possibilities.

On the other hand, when an experience violates our expectation in a negative way, it registers as a –1 in our long-term memory. This is why your spouse will always remember that you forgot your anniversary in 1998.

Alternatively, when an experience violates our expectation in a positive way, it registers as a +1 in our long-term memory—which is why your spouse remembers what you did to make up for it in 1999.

So what does this have to do with getting results when you have no power and nobody likes you? We have worked with many, many people who work in corporate functions such as IT and want very much to increase confidence and reduce anxiety for their business clients, just as we prescribe. But their desire to please leads them to make regrettable choices.

Let's say that an important person in the business comes to you, an IT leader, and describes the specifications of a solution she would like you to deliver ASAP. Here's your inner monologue: "This is an extraordinarily dumb idea.

Further, we don't have the resources for this. But I don't want to make her mad and have to explain why it's a bad idea. And I don't want my boss to get involved. Hmmm. Y'know, my team has delivered in tough situations like this one before. If I work a little magic, we can do this."

And so you say to your stakeholder, "Okay."

Using Dr. Daly's explanation of expectancy violation theory, we'll use some arithmetic to show what can happen when you get in the habit of attempting heroics in an effort to please. First, let's examine the outcome of successfully pulling off the heroics 100 percent of the time (10 times out of 10).

$$0 + 0 + 0 + 0 + 0 + 0 + 0 + 0 + 0 + 0 = 0$$

Congratulations. You didn't earn any -1s. But you burned out your team in exchange for the privilege of being taken for granted.

Now let's examine a more likely scenario: What if you are successful in pulling off the heroics 90 percent of the time (an impressive 9 times out of 10)?

$$0 + 0 + 0 + 0 + 0 + 0 + 0 + 0 + 0 - 1 = -1$$

Too bad. You've burned out your team while the client complains to others about how IT's reliability is slipping.

Finally, what if you are successful in pulling off the heroics 70 percent of the time (a more than reasonable 7 times out of 10)?

$$0 + 0 + 0 + 0 + 0 + 0 + 0 - 1 - 1 - 1 = -3$$

This is really terrible! You burned out your team while the client complains to others about how incompetent you are.

This is all about risk management. Say "No" to a client now, and he or she is likely to be annoyed. But say "Yes" and then fail to deliver and you've got an even bigger problem. So the key takeaways are:

- Avoid making commitments that will require you to kill yourself just to earn a 0 as a best-case scenario (if you're successful in pulling off heroics).
- At a minimum, make sure that you are set up to consistently and predictably earn 0s (if not better).
- Consistently look for ways to deliver an experience that violates expectations in a positive way. It never hurts to have some +1s in the bank.

Building Trust

**By Christine Malcolm, Senior Vice President,
Hospital Strategy and National Facilities,
Kaiser Foundation Health Plan and Hospitals**

At Kaiser Permanente, we're investing some $25 billion over 10 years in a massive building and refurbishing project to overhaul our medical facilities. While the funding for this program comes from each of our regions, my department, National Facilities Services, is responsible for managing the entire program. As you'd imagine, the regions want to feel confident that we're investing their money carefully—especially in the current environment. Hospital construction costs have effectively doubled between 2000 and 2007, rising 97 percent per square foot.

We may never fully eliminate the region's understandable apprehensions over our sizable capital investments. But we're working hard to earn and retain their trust. Four things have helped:

Independent and conservative cost comparisons. To ensure absolute integrity for our cost comparisons, we found an existing external benchmark on California health care construction costs, and then we had an independent consultant take our numbers and line them up against the published data. This showed that we're producing our buildings at a cost that's 9 percent lower than the California health care construction industry overall.

Transparency. All the benchmarking data in the world won't mean anything to people if they don't feel that they have a line of sight into the process. So the second thing we've focused on is complete transparency. We try to get everyone in the same room, and we hide nothing about our processes—our metrics, how we use them, where they come from, how we develop them, what data we work with, and how we get our results. We involve regional leaders (our customers) in the process as much as possible.

For example, right now we're building six hospitals, and some of the costs are coming in too high. So, for each hospital, we're getting regional leaders together in a room with our team—our estimator, our metrics people, our construction economists, our project managers, and our regional leaders. And we're saying, "Okay, let's compare these costs to our metrics. Let's figure out what the differences are. Are these explainable differences? And if they're explainable differences, can we attack the problem? What can we do to take costs out here?" We wind up taking out costs and also creating a very powerful experience for our customers. They see that we're working with legitimate numbers that have integrity down to the very detailed project level, and they also see our approach to doing the best we can to save money.

Doing our jobs well. When external parties hear about what we're doing and want to come and observe, our internal credibility gets a boost. Our buildings have been recognized for innovation and excellence by the Department of Defense, the Centers for Disease Control and Prevention, the Center for Health Care Design, the American Institute of Architects, other health care systems, and even the nation of Denmark.

Never take it personally. The regions have entrusted us as stewards of an enormous investment. Of course they're anxious. Who wouldn't be? It's easy to interpret their concern as a personal affront. But I continually tell my people that none of it is about us. And it's not about our customers in the regions, either. They're working hard to deliver world-class health care to our members and patients. Just like us.

PART 3

PROVEN STRATEGIES FOR LEADING CONVERSATIONS GROUNDED IN EMPIRICAL REALITY

✓ Whet the appetite for truth (Chapter 10).

✓ Prevent excuses before they happen (Chapter 11).

✓ Banish the fantasies and fetishes that lead to finger-pointing (Chapter 12).

✓ Treat mistakes as intellectual capital and give negative feedback that doesn't freak people out (Chapter 13).

CHAPTER 10

WHET THE APPETITE FOR TRUTH

Our team holds a lot of meetings at one of Susanna Foo's restaurants in Philadelphia. We love the food. And we love the fact that we've gotten acquainted with Susanna over time. She's a celebrity chef, and being around her is a cool experience. One day we invited her to sit down with us. We told her we wanted to learn her leadership insights. Modestly, she insisted she didn't do anything in terms of leadership that is unique or worth talking about.

"Okay, just tell us your story," we said. "How did you get in the restaurant business?"

She told us that she was born in China and grew up in Taiwan, where her father was a military man—a lieutenant general—and he instilled military discipline at home. The family had a schedule. Everyone had to be on time. Everyone had to tell the truth.

Later, she moved to the United States and married. Susanna's husband's family ran a restaurant and asked her if she would pitch in and help them with it. Even though her training and education were in library science—she has a master's degree—she agreed to help. Very early on the restaurant received a very bad review, and the family was perplexed. "Why would they do that to us?"

"I know why," Susanna offered. "The food is not good. I'm going to figure out how to fix that."

We all smiled because of the simple profundity of what she had just said so matter-of-factly. "The food is not good." Unlike Susanna, most people invent excuses and engage in mental gymnastics to avoid confronting the truth. As George Orwell observed decades ago: "To see what is in front of one's nose needs a constant struggle." But why is this the case?

For an answer, let's revisit Daniel Kahneman, whom you met in a previous chapter. As you'll recall, he won the Nobel Prize for economics in 2002. With his late colleague, Amos Tversky, Kahneman explored the systematic quirks and biases that shape human decision making. They concluded that our brains use two operating systems to guide the choices we make.

- The first system, intuition, is "fast, automatic, effortless, associative, and often emotionally charged." It's also "governed by habit and therefore difficult to control or modify." This system produces impressions that guide our choices.

- The second system, reason, is "slower, serial, effortful, and deliberately controlled." It's also "relatively flexible and potentially rule-governed." This system produces judgments that guide our choices.

We tend to think that this second system—reasoning—is in command of most of our important decisions and actions, that most of our beliefs and behaviors reflect thoughtful judgments. It turns out that this is one of those lies that our intuition system tells us. According to Kahneman, most of our choices, including the decisions we make when the stakes are high, flow from intuition rather than reasoning. But we think otherwise. Researchers have found that "the conscious brain often erroneously interprets behavior that emerges from automatic, affective processes as the outcome of cognitive deliberations."[1]

If this is accurate—that we are primarily intuition-driven but imagine ourselves reason-driven—it explains why we so confidently believe we possess truth when all we have is truthiness. This latter term—coined by satirist Stephen Colbert on the pilot episode of the *Colbert Report* and now recognized by Webster's Dictionary—refers to "the quality of preferring concepts or facts one wishes to be true to concepts or facts known to be true." In short, our intuition system, which runs on "emotionally charged" impressions, consistently favors what we wish to be true over facts known to be true because the former just feels better.

Before proceeding, we must note that our heavy reliance on intuition is not necessarily a bad thing. In many ways, it's a very good thing. Scientists believe that our intuitive ability, which equips us to react quickly under pressure and competing demands for our attention, is likely a product of natural selection. It was essential to human survival; we wouldn't be here without it. But that's not all. As Kahneman acknowledged, "There are . . . situations in which skilled decision makers do better when they trust their intuitions than when they engage in detailed analysis."[2] Malcolm Gladwell's best-seller *Blink* thoughtfully elaborated on this theme, extolling the virtues of "thinslicing" and the "power of not thinking." However, as even Gladwell made clear, your intuition also has significant limitations and can get you into trouble.[3]

So how can you improve the quality control? Kahneman says it helps "if you know statistics" and are someone who "thinks it's fun to think." But that doesn't provide you much guidance if you don't currently fall into either of those categories (or even if you do). There is, however, Kahneman suggests, something else that can help: "deliberate attention" and effort. In other words, if you want to create a culture that elevates "facts known to be true" over "facts one wishes to be true," you've actually got to work at it—because it doesn't come naturally. In the rest of this chapter, we'll explore some practical applications of this insight.

What You Need to Know (but Probably Don't)

When Dean Edwards became the chief procurement officer at Kaiser Permanente, taking on his first role in the complex world of managed health care, he knew he needed access to unfiltered information. "We committed to deliver hundreds of millions of dollars in cost savings in a relatively short period of time. You can't take on an aggressive goal like that—and succeed at it—if you're mired in wishful thinking," he told us. "Reliable information about what's working and what isn't—even if it's unpleasant—makes it possible to recalibrate as we go, to ensure the right outcome."

Early in Dean's career, he'd encountered a leader who'd asked his staff to complete a 360-degree evaluation. When he didn't like the results, the leader sent it back to the team to redo it. It made an impression on Dean. "I vowed I would never be the kind of leader who claims to want to know the truth but really doesn't have the appetite for it. Delusions are so much sweeter," he says. "But they make you very, very vulnerable." So he did a few things to make sure that he was getting the unvarnished truth—primarily by putting around him, as he described them, "people who will tell me . . . what I need to know but probably don't."

To tap into the informal networks of his organization, we helped Dean put together a communication advisory council composed of a dozen people from across the department, nominated by their peers. The first time this group came together, we facilitated and asked the members to come up with recommendations for Dean about how to improve communication. And we encouraged them to be candid. They took it seriously. So one of the things he heard was, "Dean, your e-mails suck." Instead of taking offense, Dean ate it up and subsequently took steps to improve the brevity, timeliness, and relevance of his communications. "And now my e-mails don't suck," he tells us. "Or at least, they suck less."

But what's even better is that Dean's reaction to the council's feedback told them everything they needed to know about whether the group's mission was authentic or just a new ritual designed to look good. Should they just go through the motions or really engage? After only their first session, they knew it was the latter.

Dean continues to rely heavily on the council to keep him informed about what he needs to know but probably doesn't—and for advice on what to do about it.

Another thing Dean's done, in response to input and feedback from the communication advisory council, is to launch a "day-in-the-life" program. From time to time, he goes out and spends a day with someone in the ranks. And he's charged each member of his senior team to do the same thing. "Some leaders like to do walk-arounds," Dean explains. "But when you spend only 30 seconds with someone, it's easier and safer for them to keep the conversation formal, stiff, and generally perfunctory and inauthentic. When you spend a full day with someone, it becomes informal pretty quickly, and you gain invaluable insights into what's happening that are hard to come by via any other means."

There's one other important element of Dean's strategy for putting around him people who will tell him what he needs to hear. One of the great resources for senior leaders at Kaiser Permanente is the executive consultant. The role is part lieutenant, part chief of staff, part glorified assistant, and part security blanket. When Dean informed us that he was looking for an executive consultant, we told him about a qualified candidate in another department. We'd worked with her in the past—but we warned Dean that she had once described him to us, based on a single, fleeting encounter, as "an unmitigated jackass." To Dean's mind, that didn't disqualify her from consideration; in fact, just the opposite: He immediately sought her out and hired her as his new executive consultant. It worked. By telling him what he needs to hear, even when it hurts, and critiquing his ideas, Laurie Spoon has helped Dean, as he puts it, to "stay out of my own way for over three years"—during which time Dean's organization has delivered over $400 million in hard cost savings to Kaiser Permanente.

If Trust Falls but You Don't Measure It, Does It Make a Sound? (The Answer Is Yes)

At Highmark, a major health insurer based in Pittsburgh, management has created a "Trust Index" to measure employee engagement and trust in leadership. Recently, some executives didn't want to conduct the next scheduled administration of the Trust Index because of an impending merger. According to CEO Ken Melani, "They were concerned that the merger would hurt our results, and we wouldn't look as good as we had in previous surveys." Ken's response: "Wait a second. You can't just do the surveys when times are good and not during times of uncertainty. Things happen every day. And if scores fall, we want to know so we can address those concerns."

So the company proceeded with the survey. And it turns out that the results actually were as good as or better than before the announcement of the merger. Ken was pleased. "Employees know that we're honest and we're communicating and that even in the midst of change we're not going to disengage."

Another metric Ken uses informally to gauge organizational trust is the percentage of letters and notes from the workforce that are actually signed—because the writers have no fear of reprisal. "Meaningful feedback comes in all forms—the good, the bad, and the ugly!" Ken says. And at Highmark, management wants to hear it all.

Gap Analysis: What We Say versus What We Do

Our colleagues Bill Adams and David Spach at Maxcomm specialize in, among other things, helping leaders engage their people in structured conversations to get mutually grounded in empirical reality. One way to do this is through relatively informal, face-to-face conversations with small groups of employees around the organization's stated values—what the organization claims to stand for. For each stated value, the leader guides the discussion around five questions (that are rated on a 7-point scale, where 1 means "Never see it" and 7 means "It's everywhere I look"):

1. How well are we currently living this value?
2. What are examples of this value in action?
3. What are examples of violating this value?
4. What's getting in the way of living this value?
5. What's making it easy to live this value?

For leaders willing to listen, this exercise provides the opportunity to catch small problems before they become big ones, clarify and amplify expectations, challenge employees' excuses, and identify how they (the leaders) can more effectively take away excuses and create the conditions of accountability.

Bill and David have helped leaders around the globe conduct these sessions, and the vast majority are enormously effective. To a leadership team that cares about aligning words and actions and has asserted a commitment to, say, empowerment, a comment such as "I've never been penalized for missing a deadline, but I have been for not getting a third approval" provides an unpleasant but important wake-up call.

And then you have to take action to close the gap between what the organization claims to value and what it appears to value instead. Leading without excuses requires bringing the messages and behavior into alignment. This is what Mike Rawlings did when he was president of Pizza Hut and discovered a gap.

When YUM Brands (Pizza Hut, Taco Bell, and KFC) was spun off from PepsiCo, Mike and his colleagues set out to create a values-based restaurant culture that was distinct from the PepsiCo culture. "We wanted to make 'belief in people' a key value, which makes perfect sense when you're in a people-intensive business like restaurants," he recalls.

But making the transition to putting people first when all past success had come from the Pepsi culture, which put results first, wasn't easy. "We had really strong leaders whose success and promotions had been based on delivering results, not necessarily their belief in people. It was hard for them, given their strong belief in what they were doing and their commitment to delivering results, to have to make compromises or to have the patience to take the time to develop people," Mike says.

As a result, when they launched a new 360-degree leadership survey based on the new YUM values, they faced a credibility gap. The survey asked respondents to assess their leaders', peers', and the organization's "belief in people." "But that assessment was not how we really promoted or rewarded people," Mike says. "The system was still based on the values that worked at PepsiCo: first and foremost on delivering results but also on demonstrating thought leadership and showing leadership ability and charisma."

So what did he do? "I told our chairman that we should just be intellectually honest with ourselves and capture those things in the 360. We made some changes that included 'delivering results' and the 360 process was seen as having much more credibility."

Connecting to Reality

By Joe Trippi

(Joe is best known for managing Howard Dean's 2004 campaign, whose revolutionary use of the Internet changed the way campaigns are run.)

For leaders of organizations, one of the great things about social media is that it gives you real-time access to your people in a way that you didn't have before. But that means you're going to hear some things that might make you uncomfortable. My advice: Lose your delusions—the conversation is happening even if you cover your ears.

There's real power in hearing what your employees are saying. I don't mean through focus groups and employee surveys; I mean listening to the way your employees actually talk to each other, while you host the whole thing. Maybe something isn't working the way it's supposed to, but here are all the things that could make it better. Knowing those things gives you the ability to take action on them—and sooner rather than later.

You may recall that in the middle of the 2008 presidential campaign, a lot of Obama's base was angry because he voted in the Senate in support of the bill that provided retroactive immunity to the telecoms that cooperated with the Bush administration's domestic surveillance program. In the old model, these unhappy conversations would be occurring in office cubicles, at kitchen tables, and over the neighbor's fence. In the new model, many of these conversations actually happened on Obama's Web site. Maybe that sounds crazy—providing a forum for people to criticize you.

But think about it: If those conversations were going to happen anyway, the enlightened argument is, "Why wouldn't Obama want to be the one facilitating and monitoring those conversations?" If you're willing to keep your head out of the sand, you can become a key part of those conversations. You can use them to clarify your position and hear the things you need to hear in order to respond effectively to what people are actually saying. It's better to immediately listen and engage your audiences than to wait for it to bubble up and bite you on the ass.

That's why I say: It's better to hear "You're an idiot" now than to hear it six months too late or not at all. When I was running the Dean campaign, we put 50 signs up on the Web site that people could download: "Ohio for Dean." "Alaska for Dean." "South Carolina for Dean." Once the signs were ready, we announced to the world that they could download their own file, and they no longer had to contact headquarters and wait for signs to be sent. Within three minutes, someone on our blog wrote, "You know, Joe Trippi, you're an idiot. Puerto Ricans vote in the Democratic primary, and you don't have a 'Puerto Rico for Dean' sign up." We immediately put up a "Puerto Rico for Dean" sign and apologized to the entire community. Several people quickly wrote back, "Thank you."

But then the next comment came in from London. "You're an idiot. We have six million Americans abroad for Dean. You don't have an 'Americans Abroad for Dean' sign. That's 6 million votes for the president. How could you ignore us?" Of course, the team immediately posted an "Americans Abroad for Dean" sign. The first thank-you came from a woman in Spain. All of that happened in eight minutes.

No one from Puerto Rico would have called the campaign headquarters and said, "Hey, you idiots didn't print 'Puerto Rico for Dean' signs." A call from London or Spain? Not in a million years. It would have taken months to discover the error and fix it. There are millions of people out there, but only 60 of us in the headquarters. Those people were able to scrutinize our actions and say, "Hey, you missed this" or "If you turned this that way, it would be a lot better." If you use social media smartly, you can learn quickly about problems and fix them right away.

CHAPTER 11

PREVENT EXCUSES BEFORE THEY HAPPEN

Reflecting on the financial meltdown that began in 2008, history professor Jerry Muller observed:

"This may be our first epistemologically driven depression. (Epistemology is the branch of philosophy that deals with the nature and limits of knowledge, with how we know what we think we know.) That is, a large role was played by the failure of the private and corporate actors to *understand what they were doing*. Most heads of ailing or deceased financial institutions did not comprehend the degree of risk and exposure entailed by the dealings of their underlings."[1]

Adds Nick Paumgarten: "Many of the people responsible for evaluating the [financial] engineering [that led to the crisis] considered their mystification to be further proof of its brilliance. They were, like Bernie Madoff's investors, comforted by their own ignorance."[2] This may seem shocking until you consider the *optimism bias* to which scientists say we're naturally prone. The term refers to our astounding tendency to overestimate the likelihood that good things will happen to us and to underestimate the probabilities of bad outcomes.[3]

On the one hand, taking a rosy view of the world helps to suppress your existential dread so that you can get out of bed in the morning to pursue new opportunities. Unchecked, however, it also can lead you to ignore risks and commit yourself and your team to unsound choices and actions. The French mathematician and philosopher Imre Lakatos put it eloquently: "It is perfectly rational to play a risky game: What is irrational is to deceive oneself about the risk." Or, as rapper Ice Cube put it more succinctly, you ought to "Check yourself before you wreck yourself."

No matter how smart you are, you put yourself and your organization in peril when you ignore this advice. Look at Harvard. The university depends on its endowment to fund a significant portion of its annual operating budget. For a time, the university was so confident in its investment strategy, which included exotic financial instruments, that it borrowed *above* the endowment's value to place additional bets.[4] When the stock market plunged in 2008, the university had to unload $2 billion in stock at fire-sale prices in order to cover the gamble. As of this writing, Harvard has lost $11 billion, implemented a hiring and salary freeze, and is reducing the size of its staff.

How could this happen in a place with so much intellectual firepower? As a Harvard insider told *Boston Magazine*'s Richard Bradley, "You had very smart people [here] ... who never had a real answer to the question, 'What would happen if this doesn't work out our way? What if what the black box is predicting doesn't occur?' The answer would always be, 'That's impossible' or 'You don't understand.' The arrogance was palpable."

What's the alternative? Again, the solution lies in leading conversations grounded in empirical reality. By engaging your team in an eyes-wide-open reality check prior to making a big decision, developing a strategy, and committing your resources and reputational capital toward an important effort, you can reduce the risk of delusional choices and proactively prevent excuses before they happen. In the rest of this chapter, we'll describe some practical ways to do this.

Good Old-Fashioned Debate

Political debates have become nonintellectual exercises, judged according to superficial criteria by self-appointed pundits or, more recently, scored intuitively by indecisive voters in Ohio holding hand-held dials. At Vanguard, however, the company clings to the old-fashioned belief that debates are an intellectual exercise—more specifically, that you can use debate to refine and test ideas and guide the development and validation of business strategy. To that end, the company uses "devil's advocacy sessions," where senior staff appoint teams of officers to debate opposite sides of a key business decision under consideration.

As Chairman and former Chief Executive Officer (CEO) Jack Brennan told us, "Not only do the participants have to take a stand; they have to do it with passion and conviction. Some of our best decisions—'go' or 'no go'—have come out of these sessions."

Sounding Board: "Do We Really, Really Want to Initiate This Project?"

To keep optimism bias in check, IBM developed a process to scrutinize possible projects. Heike Bruch and Sumantra Ghoshal tell the story in a terrific book called, *A Bias for Action*.[5] The head of a European subsidiary of IBM, Sven Olafson, noticed "many activities that were started with great enthusiasm at IBM [that] were often completed half-heartedly or abandoned halfway."[6]

So the company began requiring its managers to present all new projects to a "Sounding Board" responsible for approving projects, prioritizing them, and allocating re-sources. Sven quickly noticed two things: First, every proposal offered overly optimistic projections of the time and resources required, and second, the managers all focused solely on the business case for each project and never analyzed the personal stakes required to complete it. So he revised the process and required that each proposal address four factors:

- Business gains
- Business risks
- Personal advantages
- Personal disadvantages

On top of that, he required every manager who proposed a project to answer questions such as

- What would it cost me personally to undertake this project?
- What must I stop doing in order to have the time to do this?
- What else would I do if I didn't take up this project?

Even after the board actually approved a proposal, its leader would ask one more time whether the manager who brought it forward really wanted to take it on. This final verbal commitment sealed the deal.

As a result, the number of projects launched dropped dramatically, and the company successfully completed 95 percent of those it started. In short, by discouraging optimism-biased decision making, the "Sounding Board" promoted intellectual honesty and a healthy respect for empirical reality.

Going in Eyes Wide Open with Force-Field Analysis

Force-field analysis was developed by social psychologist Kurt Lewin decades ago and was popularized more recently by Six Sigma enthusiasts. In our version of force-field analysis, we bring together a team that has already made the decision to embark on some significant project, initiative, or other effort. With those assembled, we facilitate an in-depth discussion around two questions:

What are all the things (people, habits, situational factors, etc.) that are working against your success? What's going to make it hard to succeed? The point is to create a complete list of all the things that will become excuses later if the team fails to address or plan for them now. Toward that end, we typically work with the group to prioritize the forces working against them (as they've listed them) and help them determine strategies to mitigate or eliminate those factors.

What are all the things (people, habits, situational factors, etc.) that are working in your favor? What's going to help you succeed? There are a couple of reasons for asking this question. The most obvious is to inventory the positive forces the group can leverage in the pursuit of its goals. The second point is to provide perspective. Most groups have just as many factors working for them as against them— and making that fact explicit helps to minimize whining.

Here's an example of the tool in action: A well-known German manufacturer was about to implement a new performance management program at the same time that it was closing plants. We recommended that, as part of the rollout, the executive committee bring the site managers together and conduct a force-field analysis.

First, the group listed the forces that would work against the success of the new program—such as

- Employees here often see hard work as an acceptable substitute for actual results.
- Not everyone understands the reasons for the changes we're making.
- We say we're paying for performance, but people feel like they aren't seeing the money.

With factors like these made explicit, the new CEO, the rest of the executive committee, and the site managers were able to have an eyes-wide-open discussion about what it would take to address and overcome these challenges in a proactive and more comprehensive way (instead of waiting and then reacting to each as it bubbled to the surface).

Next, we asked the group to list the forces that were working in their favor, which included these:

- We attract talented, high-performing people to work here.

- Even if we've had a lot of turnover on the executive level, our people at other levels in the organization have demonstrated their loyalty, and they matter to us.
- We have a lot of managers with decades of experience, and we can draw on their accumulated knowledge.

The second discussion focused on how to take advantage of these factors and offered a balanced perspective. Yes, the company needed to openly recognize and confront some tough challenges—but it also needed to acknowledge that it enjoyed some factors working in its favor that it shouldn't take for granted.

Clear Critical Pathways

By Bob Sturmer, a process-improvement expert at one of the top-ranked hospitals in the United States

Every project has a *critical path* that is associated with project success. This is the sequence of tasks where bottlenecks are likely to occur and throw a project off schedule or stop it dead in its tracks.

Executives and managers often misuse the term *critical path* to mean "a really important set of tasks that we must get done." That description, however, masks its intended use as a valuable risk-mitigating tool because it simplifies its meaning to emphasize only task *importance*—when the essential issue is really task *dependency*.

To illustrate critical path, let's use a simple project like cooking a spaghetti dinner. You've invited a friend to your house at 6:30 p.m. for dinner with the intention of making an eight o'clock movie. An hour before your guest arrives, you prepared vegetables for your side dish and sautéed the garlic and onions for the sauce. You set the table, open the wine, and the doorbell rings. You greet your guest, pour the wine, and return to the kitchen to make the pasta when you realize . . . no boiling water for the pasta. You quickly fill the pot and crank the heat. About 30 minutes pass, your side dish is ruined, and you're running out of time and wine. Maybe you should have had a pizza delivered.

Sure, you performed all the "really important tasks," but you neglected to consider the timing of a simple activity—and it spoiled what otherwise would have been a great dinner.

The solution is to ask in advance.

- Are there any pots of water that require boiling? Or, in a business context, what parts of this project are potential bottlenecks because of resource, time, or material constraints?
- How can we direct resources toward there to prevent bottlenecks?

Here's an example: A large pharmaceutical company wanted to use a new multimillion-dollar content-management system to support its drug application process and use it for a submission for one of its final-phase drugs for Food and Drug Administration (FDA) approval. The scheduled "go-live" was suddenly in jeopardy when during the last phases of testing someone discovered a bug in one of the recently released software components touted as ready for market by a vendor. All resources were allocated to this planned final phase but could not move forward because of this unanticipated problem. As Warren Buffett says, "[Y]ou can't produce a baby in one month by getting nine women pregnant." It took four weeks for an analyst to evaluate the company's options and implement a revised plan before resources could resume the final testing and production installation of the system. The industry benchmark is that you lose $1 million in revenue for every week a drug isn't yet on the market. So you do the math. During the planning stage, project leaders could have added steps in the plan to test that risky software component in parallel with an earlier development phase. The 40 hours added to the budget, in hindsight, would have produced enormous return on investment.

Crystal Ball

Why did the vast majority of bankers, regulators, policy-makers, and economists fail to foresee the housing bubble bursting and the associated wreckage to the economy? It's remarkable, says Wharton Management Professor Sidney G. Winter, "that serious people were willing to commit, both intellectually and financially, to the idea that housing prices would rise indefinitely, a really bizarre idea considering the commonsense fact that home prices could not continue rising faster than household incomes."[7]

It's a pity that none of those "serious people" ever got together to perform a *crystal-ball exercise*, which is one of our favorite tools for validating confidence and confronting the stuff people may not know (or may be pretending not to know).

Marvin Cohen, Jared Freeman, and Bryan Thompson developed the exercise in the 1990s as a way to train Army officers to test key assumptions before executing important decisions.[8] Imagine that a battalion officer knows an enemy force is across the river. He formulates a response based on his assumption that the enemy will cross the river at a particular point (point X). Why point X? Because the battalion officer knows the water there is shallow and the surrounding vegetation provides cover. Makes sense. But the stakes are high: Preparations to meet and defeat the enemy will succeed or fail based on the accuracy of the assumption that the enemy will come across at point X.

To test this critical assumption, the officer and his team "imagine that a perfect intelligence source, such as a crystal ball, tells [them that they're] wrong." Unfortunately, the crystal ball doesn't reveal what alternative action the enemy takes, but it's "crystal clear" that they're not crossing at point X. The officer and his team then try to explain why their core assumption was wrong. What could lead the enemy to do something other than cross the river at what seems like a relatively obvious location?

According to Cohen and his colleagues, trainees are usually "surprised at the quantity and the plausibility of the exceptions that the crystal ball elicits from them." For example, the enemy might

- Anticipate that our force will be at point X and decide not to cross there.
- Detect the movement of our force to point X and decide not to cross there.
- Cross at another good site we don't know about.
- Not know how good a location point X is.
- Not have any river-crossing assets and can't cross.
- Have river-crossing assets so good that they can cross elsewhere.
- Have a large enough force that they can accept casualties in crossing elsewhere.
- Have different objectives than we think and don't need to cross the river at all.

Next, they consider each of these assumption-undermining possibilities, at least briefly. They might dismiss some as implausible ("There's no way they can accept large casualities."). They can debate the relative likelihood of each plausible exception ("Really, how confident are we that point X is the only good site and that there isn't another we don't know about?"). They can decide to gather more intelligence, develop contingency plans, or revise their strategy entirely. Or they might decide to accept some known risks, stick with their previous assumption that the enemy is most likely to cross at point X (imaginary crystal ball be damned), and proceed accordingly. As Cohen and his colleagues point out, "In the end, even if officers retain the original strategy, their confidence in it will have been *earned* [emphasis ours]."

We've used the crystal-ball exercise with clients in a variety of high-stakes situations, helping them to validate their operating assumptions and confront what they don't know or may be pretending not to know. This is especially important to do in the early stages of a major business initiative.

It's important to get the right people in the room to ensure diversity of perspective. It's also important to have an outside facilitator—which probably sounds like a self-serving thing for us to say. However, here's why it's so critical: As Karl Weick and Kathleen Sutcliffe noted in their book on high-reliability decision making in nuclear power plants and on aircraft carriers, "[D]iverse views typically are disproportionately distributed toward the bottom of the organization, which means that those most likely to catch unanticipated warning signals have the least power and argumentative skill to persuade others that [a potential issue] should be taken seriously."[9] In most settings, only a skilled outside facilitator can elicit candid, unfiltered input from the people in the room who possess the least amount of positional power.

We might start off the exercise by saying, "Okay, you're moving forward with your current implementation strategy, recognizing that your reputations and the organization's resources are on the line. So I'm looking into my crystal ball, and it gives me a very clear and accurate picture of what's happening one year from today. And unfortunately, it's telling me that this initiative is behind schedule, over budget, and failing to deliver the promised benefits. Sadly, the crystal ball doesn't tell me why."

Then we ask the participants to *independently* write down at least three things that could lead to the outcomes the crystal ball is describing. (The independent idea generation helps to ensure that the most powerful person in the room doesn't have a chilling effect on the input of the other participants.) Then we ask each person in the room to read one item from his or her list, and we go around the room in multiple rounds until we've captured all the unique ideas. A typical list might include such things as:

- The CEO's real support is tepid; when key stakeholders start pushing back, she'll withdraw political support.
- Our key stakeholders don't really understand what this will require of them, so their current buy-in doesn't mean much.
- We can't recruit enough "A" players on the project team because they're needed in their current roles.

- We brought in a consulting firm that doesn't really understand our culture and how we're different from their previous clients.
- Business performance will decline and we won't have the budget to complete the initiative.
- Technology integration turns out to be an even bigger challenge than we think.
- Turnover in the C-suite changes priorities and the political landscape.

Then we ask each participant—again, independently—to assign a probability rating to each of these issues on a 0 to 100 scale, where 0 means "No way this happens" and 100 means "It's certain to occur." After participants report their ratings, we identify the range of responses and median ratings for each issue. Then we lead a structured discussion. First, we explore the issues that elicited the most diverse range of ratings. "Tom, you think there's an 80 percent chance that technology integration is going to be tougher than the current plan anticipates. Deb, you said there's only a 10 percent chance that's going to happen. I'd like each of you to take two minutes to explain your thinking." This is where we're most likely to surface the stuff that people have been pretending not to know—and sometimes it can get heated, as in "C'mon guys! What evidence do we really have that the CEO is genuinely committed to seeing this through?"

After that, we give participants an opportunity to change their 0 to 100 likelihood ratings for each issue. Then we order the issues from most to least likely (based on median ratings) and lead discussions on how to tackle each. Something good always comes out of these discussions. Sometimes it involves merely tweaking or fortifying the implementation strategy, for example, adjusting the timeline, taking steps to reduce risks, or other things. Occasionally, the team decides to accept the known risks and proceed as originally planned— but with more "earned confidence" than it previously possessed. And more than once, the crystal-ball exercise has provided the impetus for our clients to cancel or significantly rescope an initiative that they've come to realize is, if not doomed, not worth the considerable risks to which they've now become enlightened. Making this decision usually involves some loss of face—but most of our clients would agree that it's better to fail gracefully now than spectacularly later. And this is why we say that some of the work we're most proud of has involved helping our clients decide to *not* do something.

When a Project's in Progress, Ask Forward-Facing Questions

Steve McQueen tells a joke in *The Magnificent Seven* about a guy who's falling off a building. As he flies by a window, someone yells, "How ya' doin'?" The response is "So far, so good!"

According to our colleague, process guru Harold Strawbridge, that's a descriptive project status from this moment backward. And, he says, it's fine to look back when your aim is to reward progress and recognize accomplishments. But you must look forward to assess and monitor where you are and where you need to be. At any given point in time, a project will succeed based only on what you do with the time remaining.

So he recommends that leaders ask questions throughout the course of a project to prevent excuses before they happen:

1. What are the barriers to meeting the next project milestone?
2. What issues do we have regarding materials . . . or people . . . or process . . . or technology?
3. What have we discovered about doing this project that we should keep doing?
4. What have we discovered that we have to stop doing?
5. What criteria have we established to measure our progress?

"Asking these questions will elicit information about things that require action from this point forward in the project," Harold says. For each issue identified, the natural follow-up is, "So what are we going to do about it?" which begets, "Who's going to do that and when will it be done?"

"Now you're about the job of making actionable future steps visible," Harold says. "Once the steps are visible, it's easier to clarify expectations around them, and subsequently easier for the project team to hit the target."

Jim Rohr, CEO, PNC Bank: "Love Your Balance Sheet: Someday You Will Meet It"

(With our colleague Lilly Linton, we interviewed Jim Rohr, CEO of the fifth largest bank in the United States, in July 2008, just a couple of months before Wall Street "collapsed." Jim's insights and observations proved prescient.)

When I joined the training program here some years ago, all I wanted to do was sell. I was convinced that getting out of the training program and in front of clients would establish me as a performer. And I wanted to be a performer. So I lobbied to have them accelerate the credit risk portion of the training. Looking back, if some trainee were to say that to me today, I'd say that he or she doesn't have a very bright future in banking.

Why? Because at the end of the day, we are in the risk-management business. Risk management is everybody's job. We've gone across the entire company and asked every one of our 28,000 employees to spend time thinking about how their work impacts our risk profile. Everyone in each one of our businesses has capital allocated based on risks. So they have to think about risk every time they make a strategic decision. It starts with reports that go to the board and the executive management team and the risk committee, and it goes all the way down through the company. It took us a while, but I can tell you that it is working well.

We have 28,000 people, and no matter what happens, we're operating as a team—we're working together to manage risk . . . and by extension, serve the customer and shareholders. That's the key to our success.

That perspective also explains why we like to have multiple revenue drivers. More than half our earnings come from fee-based components rather than interest income, which is more volatile.

We—in the banking industry as a whole—have to be much better prepared. We have to understand what is on our balance sheet. We have to understand our liability structure better, and we have to have better contingency plans for what happens to the liquidity should certain things change.

We need a governance structure that forces us to understand the profitability of certain activities and allocate capital and pay the right way. That's going to be a struggle, and it is something that we clearly have to get right—not only as individual organizations but also as an industry.

Thirty-five years ago, a manager of our credit committee said to me: "Remember, love your balance sheet. Some day you will meet it." I didn't have any idea what he was talking about then, but I know now. When we put loans on our books, we won't know for two or three years if they're good loans. That's why you stick to the fundamentals. Know your borrower. Know your customer. Know your balance sheet. Those are basic tenets of banking.

CHAPTER 12

BANISH THE FANTASIES AND FETISHES THAT LEAD TO FINGERPOINTING

Narcissistic romanticism in the workplace is embarrassing and cringe inducing. More important, when it goes unchecked, it leads to fingerpointing and excuse making. Here are four common fantasies in which you cannot allow yourself or your people to indulge—if you want to have a disciplined culture where accountability and performance are consistently high.

Good Crop, Bad Crop

Who deserves the credit when things go well? Who deserves the blame when they don't? A phenomenon social scientists call *self-serving bias* makes it easy for us to answer "me" and "not me," respectively.[1,2] *Self-serving bias* refers to our tendency to take credit for successes but to chalk up failures to factors outside our control (such as bad luck or other external variables).[3] For example, what happens when my kid gets a scholarship to a top college? It's all the evidence I need to convince me I'm a great parent. But when my kid goes to jail? She hung out with the wrong friends and had crummy teachers. What could I do?

Employees exhibit self-serving bias all the time. They like to take credit, sometimes supersized credit, for successes ("I saved the day on this project. My boss should be kissing my feet"), but they often shun responsibility for failures ("I know I said I'd do it, but people kept bugging me with other stuff").

Of course, leaders exhibit self-serving bias, too. In fact, lots of it, as Sydney Finkelstein found in his assessment entitled, *Why Smart Executives Fail*. "In one organization we studied," he says, "the CEO spent the entire 45-minute interview explaining all the reasons why others were to blame for the calamity that hit his company. Regulators, customers, the government, and even other executives within the firm—all were responsible. No mention was made, however, of personal culpability."[4]

There's a tongue-in-cheek saying among old Communist party bosses: "Good crops come from good farming; bad crops come from bad weather." Our cold war policy of containment stopped the spread of their ideology across our borders but did little to prevent us from producing our own homegrown version of "good crop/bad crop" thinking.

Even before the Wall Street bailout, our research shows that employees didn't care that much about executive compensation per se; what they resent is a policy of "socialism in the C-suite, capitalism for the rest of you"—whereby senior executives grant themselves all the positive consequences of success while shielding themselves from the negative consequences of failure.

E. L. Kersten, the satirist and evil genius who made his name making fun of Successories posters, lampooned this tendency in his masterpiece, *The Art of Demotivation:*

It is important that the variable pay for executives not be contingent upon the financial performance of the company, and instead that it be based upon a variety of factors such as tenure, popularity with the board, or something similar. We all know that the financial performance of a company is not always an accurate indicator of an executive's enduring value or contribution, and therefore executives should not be punished for leading their companies through the turbulent seas of financial difficulty. In fact, periods of financial difficulty may even warrant additional, unexpected perks or compensation as a way of showing gratitude for an executive's leadership during difficult times.[5]

"When I wrote that, I couldn't have imagined the post-bailout AIG spa weekend," Kersten told us recently, referring to the pampering to which executives of the giant insurance company treated themselves soon after it failed. "As they say, sometimes life imitates art."

Writer Nick Paumgarten is less amused:

> In congressional testimony, the disgraced CEOs of failed institutions—Richard Fuld, of Lehman Brothers; Martin Sullivan, of AIG—talked about a "financial tsunami" that caught them unaware, as though they had not figured in the plate tectonics. . . . but the potential for catastrophe was clear to see, for all who had eyes to see it, and men like Fuld and Sullivan were paid tens of millions of dollars to have or hire such eyes. . . . So to claim ignorance or helplessness is to admit to negligence, or to tell a lie. It grated when, last fall, Donald Trump tried to get out of paying debts by claiming that the economic meltdown was a "force majeure"—the legal equivalent, basically, of an act of God—and not a logical outcome of a set of observable circumstances. The real-estate bubble was not a great secret.[6]

What would accountability for bailed-out bankers look like? "I want them poor, and they deserve to be poor," says *Black Swan* author Nassim Taleb. "You can't have capitalism without punishment."[7]

That's not something they want to hear in the fantasy bubble inhabited by people like the executive at bailout-recipient Citigroup, who wrote to colleagues: "No offense to Middle America, but if someone went to Columbia or

Wharton, [even if] their company is a fumbling, mismanaged bank, why should they all of a sudden be paid the same as the guy down the block who delivers restaurant supplies for Sysco out of a huge, shiny truck?"[8]

So what can you do in your own sphere of influence to keep the "good crop/bad crop" mentality in check? Besides leading by example, you can call it out when you see your employees exhibiting this bias (and invite them to point it out when they perceive you are doing the same thing). Rita Johnson, an executive from McDonald's Leadership Institute, described to us her "lesson learned."

"At McDonald's, spending time working as a store manager in the restaurants is typically part of the career path. And I learned a lot, including some insights about leading without excuses," she says.

At McDonald's, quality, service, cleanliness, and value (QSC&V) are the foundations of the organization on which the company bases everything else. "We continuously measure those four variables. If you can't deliver quality, service, cleanliness, and value on a day-to-day basis to your customers, you're not going to be successful in the long term, and everybody knows that."

So one day Rita's supervisor came to visit. He said, "You know, the QSC levels in your restaurant are really, really good. And they have been for some time. To what do you credit that?"

And Rita said, "Oh, because I keep people focused on it, and we work really hard here."

And then he said: "So why are sales down?"

Rita said, "Oh, I have no idea. But I think it has a lot to do with the competition down the street."

The supervisor said to Rita, "Hmm. Whenever I ask you why things are up, you say it's all just because of what you did as a leader. But whenever sales are down, it must be the competition, or a road closure down the street, or it's been raining a lot. But it's never you as a leader."

"It's the kind of insight you tend not to forget," Rita says. "And that's what's so great about the way we grow leaders at McDonald's. The restaurant experience isn't just about learning operations—it includes many other leadership lessons, too."

Another way to compensate for self-serving bias and lead by example is to err on the side of giving too much credit to others and too little to yourself. It's a sign of a confident leader. It draws followers to you and builds loyalty and trust. For some leaders we know, this orientation comes naturally. An example is Lincoln Financial Distributors CEO Terry Mullen, who said: "I don't need to take the credit. I try whenever I can to give it to somebody else because they are the ones actually doing the work. Honestly, I don't actually do anything. My job is to set the direction and provide leadership, then let everybody else do it. So they should be the ones to get credit for it."

Vanguard Chairman and former CEO Jack Brennan shares a similar philosophy on taking credit:

> There's an expression I use all the time, which is: "Leaders should accept all the blame and distribute all the credit." Because being a leader is credit enough. And it is putting your team front and center. It is desperately working to give your team members exposure. So if you bring in a couple of people from your team to report out on something important and you start talking, I'll say, "What are you doing? Did you do all the work? You sit over there and let somebody else talk. I want to hear from the two young people on your team." I have had that conversation a hundred times.

Another CEO who leads by example is Aetna's Ron Williams. "He's the hardest working person in the company," says his colleague Elease Wright. During Ron's first year in the company, he was asked by the then CEO to rate his own performance on a five-point scale. Ron rated himself a two because he didn't achieve all that he'd hoped to. "The former CEO said [that] he would have rated him a six if there had been such a rating," Elease told us. "So you see, Ron has a level of humility. And it shows in the way in which he interacts with people and the level of respect he has for others."

Some Guys Have All the Luck*

By Joe Nocera

(This article from the *New York Times* compares two different CEOs and illustrates the advantages of avoiding "good crop/bad crop" thinking.)

New York Times, May 24, 2008

The Dallas–Fort Worth area is home to two of the biggest U.S. airlines, American and Southwest, and for years they have both held their annual meetings on the same day. This year was no exception: Wednesday was the big day.

The American meeting started first, at 8 a.m. An hour before it began, members of the Association of Professional Flight Attendants and the Allied Pilots Association—the latter is in the midst of brutal contract negotiations with the company—began picketing.

The meeting itself could not have been more downbeat. "The U.S. airline industry as it is constituted today was not built for $125- or $130-per-barrel oil," complained Gerard Arpey, the chief executive of AMR, American's parent company.

The Southwest Airlines meeting began a few hours later. It maintains a healthy balance sheet and has plenty of cash. Its annual meetings tend to be love fests.

This year, though, was the love fest to end them all. The company's beloved cofounder, Herbert Kelleher—known to one and all as Herb—was stepping down as chairman after 37 years.

When Kelleher, 77, entered the main meeting room, shareholders gave him the kind of standing ovation usually reserved for rock stars. The Southwest pilots' union is also negotiating a new contract with management. But not only did the Southwest pilots not set up a picket line, they took out a full-page advertisement in *USA Today* thanking Kelleher for all he had done. "It has been an honor and a privilege to be a part of his aviation legacy," union President Carl Kowitzky said in a statement.

When [Kelleher] brought up the pilots' ad—and when he talked about how much the company's employees meant to him—he wept. "I'm Lucky Herbie for having all of these years with all of you," he said.

As he stepped away from the company this week, his line didn't change. "We've never had layoffs," he told me the day before the annual meeting, sitting on the couch of the single messiest executive office I've ever seen. "We could have made more money if we furloughed people. But we don't do that. And we honor them constantly. They know that we value them as people, not just cogs in a machine."

Can it really be that simple?

Actually, that depends on who you ask. According to Robert Crandall, the curmudgeonly former chief executive of American Airlines—and a man who fought many a battle with Kelleher—the answer is no. "Herb has done an excellent job of sustaining a high level of employee morale and sticking to their strategy," he said. But in the next breath, he attributed Southwest's success to the fact that it was allowed to operate out of Love Field in the heart of Dallas, instead of having to move to Dallas–Fort Worth International Airport, far outside the city, like all the other airlines. "If he hadn't had the Love Field advantage, the story would have turned out differently," he grumbled.

Arsonist Firefighter

As arson investigators will attest, many times the culprit is a firefighter, often one who is highly trained.[9] When there's not enough action, arsonist firefighters start fires just so they can do what they're good at: being the hero by putting them out. In organizations, "arsonist firefighters" do the same thing. They create or perpetuate problems and drama so that they can do what they're good at: being the hero by handling the crisis (or supposed crisis, as it were). As one executive told us, "We have a lot of people who show up to work, set themselves on fire, then spend the rest of the day putting it out."

With arsonist firefighters, it's difficult to fix systemic problems and drive large-scale organizational improvements. While they pretend they have a passion for solving problems, the arsonist is really in love with the drama and is constantly looking for opportunities for further heroics. Narcissism is the core problem here; force the arsonist to simply manage things with quiet efficiency, and it destroys his or her carefully cultivated heroic self-image.

How do you manage the arsonist firefighter? It goes back to something we said in an earlier chapter. If you are rewarding or even just tolerating gratuitous heroics, you can expect to see more of them.

The challenge, of course, is that there are times when heroics and a sense of urgency are necessary. Dr. Pepper/Snapple executive Randy Gier told us how he strikes a balance.

"A lot of people can create a sense of urgency through what I call assertive adversity, in other words, creating a sense of crisis: We're $40 million behind plan; earnings are due; if we don't hit those numbers, the stock's going to tank; etc. It's not my preferred method, but it works," he says. "People will rise to the occasion. In fact, they like rising to the occasion; they like being a hero—the fireman who comes in and puts out the fire—because it provides immediate gratification and satisfaction."

But, he adds: "The problem is that it doesn't stick. If there's a new crisis every week, and every month, it gets old. People stop listening. They get crisis fatigue, and say, 'So what?' And their performance slows down."

The challenge, then, he says, is to create and sustain a sense of urgency without everything always having to be in crisis. "We do that at Doctor Pepper/Snapple by creating deadlines—but deadlines tied to the business cycle, to consumer behavior. For example, with product launches, if I'm launching a new tea, and I know that 60 percent of the business is during the summer, that's an immovable deadline. Or if we know that if we don't hit a date, Wal-Mart is not going to slot us with the shelf space we need, that's a real deadline—with Wal-Mart, you're in on time or you're out. It's not movable." By pushing for heroics only when truly necessary, Randy gets the extra energy and creativity from his people when he really needs it.

The Martyr

While arsonist firefighters create unnecessary crises, their close cousins, the martyrs, demonstrate their character and commitment by killing themselves, working all the time, and forgoing sleep. They make a fetish of being busy. But research is piling up to suggest that this lifestyle makes these martyrs sick, stupid, and forgetful. What's more, martyrs are not very fun to work with. They tend to point fingers at others who don't seem to share their commitment (as evidenced by the fact that they leave the office before them; they're unlikely to consider the possibility that it's because they're more efficient and effective at completing their work). Of course, all this ultimately hurts performance.

"Research shows that the average person needs seven to nine hours of sleep per night. Less sleep than that leads to numerous physical problems, including reduced performance, depression, anxiety, shorter temper, heart disease, risk for diabetes, and shorter life span," says Dr. Jeff Kaplan, president of The Habit Change Company, which advises organizations on wellness programs. "A study conducted by The University of Chicago's Medical Center showed that reducing eight hours of sleep to four hours of sleep each night produced changes in glucose tolerance and endocrine functioning resembling the effects of advanced age or the early stages of diabetes—after less than one week!" Kaplan also notes that lack of sleep was one of the factors that caused Chernobyl, the *Exxon Valdez* disaster, and the *Challenger* space shuttle explosion.[10]

But the martyr doesn't want to hear about any of this. He's fried, and he'll freak out on you—and see it as a personal attack. Indeed, despite all the recent research on the negative side effects of martyrdom, ". . . the attitude toward sleep and sleepiness has changed very little," says Mark W. Mahowald, director of the Minnesota Regional Sleep Disorders Center. "You never brag about how much you got, but people brag all the time about how little they got. The less sleep you get by with, the more tireless, loyal, and dedicated of a worker you are."[11]

Here's an allegory that illustrates some of the dynamics of the problem and why martyrdom is such a hard habit to break:

A consultant, we'll call him J, was coauthoring a book. One day, J's brother Greg phoned. The two normally rode their bikes together at least 50 miles per week. Greg was calling to express concern, pointing out to J that he hadn't been on his road bike for two months. J, who was busily cranking away at the manuscript and had barely slept or exercised in weeks, looked down from his laptop at his gut creeping farther and farther over his belt. And so he agreed that he should take a break to join Greg for a Saturday afternoon ride of 20 miles.

Greg was a couple of weeks away from a 200-mile endurance ride for which he'd been training for months. So he'd already put in 50+ miles earlier in the day before J joined him. The two brothers set off on one of their regular routes, which included a steep hill, rising nearly 1,000 feet in less than a mile. Halfway through the climb, J completely lost his breath. Meanwhile, Greg was talking and breathing regularly, maintaining an efficient, sustainable pace.

Suddenly, an enormous, snarling black dog raced toward the cyclists from a nearby porch. Though moments before J had nearly reached his physical limits, the threat of a vicious canine coming after him provoked an adrenaline response, and he found the energy to pump a little faster up the hill.

Just fast enough that J reached the boundaries of the dog's imagined territory before the dog reached J, and the dog retreated.

J looked back and realized Greg was standing in the road, straddling his bike, not far from the spot he'd been when the dog first charged toward them. "Dude, what are you doing?" J asked.

"Dude, what are *you* doing?" Greg replied. "You were about to drop over dead, Kujo comes after you, and you try to outrun him *uphill*?"

"Yeah, I guess that made no sense," J conceded. "What did you do?"

"Well, first, I figured that since you're out of shape and slow, he was going to chase *you*. And that proved correct. But I pulled out my water bottle to throw at him or squirt him, if necessary. And I figured if I had to outrun him, I'd improve my odds by turning around and riding *downhill*."

Both the brothers had PowerTaps on their bikes that display performance metrics, including wattage output. "Wow, I maxed out at about 900 watts coming up the hill," said J, still catching his breath, after Greg joined him. J could sustain 900 watts for all of about two seconds. Greg looked down at his readout. "I maxed out at 230 watts, he said, a level of output that a few weeks later he would sustain for 18 hours and 200 miles.

At a stop sign a few miles later, J turned and said, "I've been thinking. I've got to use this in my book. It's an example of how, when you burn yourself out, you lose access to your executive function and the ability to reason. My reptile brain helped me find the extra superhuman strength I needed to get out of danger. But it actually made no sense."

"On the other hand," J continued, "you're cool and efficient. You actually had the presence of mind to come up with a strategy. You didn't try to outrun a dog attack by riding *up* a steep hill. You're the model of what leaders need to promote and reward."

The brothers rode farther, and then Greg said, "Hey, I thought about it. Don't use the story in the book. It makes me sound nerdy while glorifying your stupidity." What a great insight, J thought, committing himself to ignore his brother's wishes. Greg had confronted a threat, and he responded with cool efficiency. No drama. No narcissistic story to tell others afterward. For the slow, out-of-shape, and stupid guy, just the opposite.

We know of far too many organizations that reward the people who flee dogs by cranking uphill. We know people who have been dinged on their performance reviews because they're never still at the office at 10 p.m. and never send e-mails at 4 a.m. They get results, but they do so with quiet efficiency rather than last-minute heroics and therefore are seen as not part of the team or sufficiently appreciative of its culture. Once again, this is where you as a leader make all the difference, based on whether you are more inclined to reward and tolerate the kind of work habits that bring momentary drama and glory or those that produce no drama but are sustainable in the long term.

Fetishes in the Workplace?

When we talk of *fetishes*, we're speaking of objects of "unreasonably excessive attention or reverence," as defined by the *American Heritage Dictionary*.[12] Here are the five fetishes we see frequently in organizations that, unchecked, hurt long-term performance and accountability. Like Aristotle, we wish only to promote "moderation in all things."

1. Personal Responsibility

Of course, personal responsibility is a good thing, because taking personal responsibility is the primary antidote to excuse making.

But not when you make a fetish of it. Malcolm Gladwell, author of *The Tipping Point* and *Blink*, notes that ". . . making a fetish of personal accountability conveniently removes the need for institutional accountability. (We court martial the grunts who abuse prisoners, not the commanding officers who let the abuse happen.) To acknowledge that the causes of [someone's] actions are complex and muddy seems permissive, and permissiveness is the hallmark of an ideology now firmly in disgrace."[13]

How does the fetish lead to fingerpointing? The easiest thing in the world for a leader to do is admonish everyone to "be accountable" and "own" all the organization's problems. But if that's not accompanied by a systematic effort to create the conditions of accountability at the institutional level, even your very best people are going to find it challenging to translate those rather empty words into action. And your save-ables are going to get tired of looking and feeling like sinners . . . and they'll look for salvation/employment elsewhere.

2. Numbers and Quantitative Measurement
Of course, numbers and quantitative measurement are good things because you need them to create clear and credible expectations. Further, you need to be able to align consequences with performance by measuring it.

But not when you make a fetish of them. Much of the time, what is easy to measure is not what's important to measure. Plus: Too many leaders attribute mystical qualities to numbers, quantitative measurements, and methodologies, even when it isn't warranted. In our recent assessment, only 75 percent of leaders who routinely use measurements can explain the difference between correlation and causality. Fewer than 25 percent can explain the conditions under which you can reasonably infer the latter. Fewer than 10 percent can explain randomness and how to take it into account when interpreting measurement results. (*Did we really conduct an assessment?* Yes, and it has roughly as much reliability as the measures and methodologies used by most business book authors.)

How does the fetish lead to fingerpointing? When your approach to measurement is dubious, you equip people to (1) take the results seriously when they are favorable but (2) discount them when they aren't. If business performance measurement is a significant part of what you're paid to do and you haven't read Nassim Taleb's *Fooled by Randomness* and Phil Rosenzweig's *Halo Effect*, you're committing professional malpractice. If you want a brief but thorough primer on the logic of correlation versus causality (and all the things that can get in the way of demonstrating the latter), and if you have $55 to spend on a thin, 45-year-old paperback, check out Donald Campbell and Julian Stanley's *Experimental and Quasi-Experimental Designs for Research*.

3. Jack Welch

Of course, Jack Welch is a good thing because he demonstrated an ability to create accountability and deliver results, and there's always something to be learned from leaders who can pull that off.

But not when you make a fetish of him. When a famous leader's formulas become a substitute for (rather than a supplement to) your own judgment, you're in trouble. Especially when you fail to take into account the context in which the famous leader made those formulas work. Here's an example from an incredulous senior executive, "I just got the word that we are to immediately put in place a yank-and-rank system to take out the bottom 10 percent because that's what GE does. Great. But 60 percent of our employees haven't had a performance review in two years. *I'm sure this will go smoothly.*"

How does the fetish lead to fingerpointing? When your application (or misapplication) of the celebrity CEO's best practices fails, you've got a ready-made excuse: "Hey, don't look at me. We just did what Jack Welch does." And with each successive rollout of the next celebrity CEO–driven fad *du jour*, your employees become more incredulous and secretly rejoice when you fail to achieve Jack Welch–like results.

4. Process and Methodology

Of course, process and methodology are good things because following processes allows people to get things done in a way that is predictable, stable, repeatable, and, if the processes are well designed, efficient.

But not when you make a fetish of them. Process and methodology (e.g., Six Sigma, Agile, etc.) purists are some of the most annoying people on earth. For them, the means to an end are the only "end" that matters—even if they compromise results.

How does the fetish lead to fingerpointing? It's said that if you gouge out the eyes of a Six Sigma purist, no jury will convict you.

5. Results

Of course, results are a good thing because that's ultimately why we're in business, right?

But not when you make a fetish of it. If you focus only on results, you can create an environment in which people seek to achieve the ends by any means necessary. And that can create ethical, reputational, and legal problems. But that's not the only point we want to make here. We live and operate in a complex and more-random-than-we'd-like-to-believe world where employees can do all the things they're supposed to do and still not get the results you seek. Then what? Do you focus only on the results or take a more nuanced perspective, recognizing that all business is a probabilistic exercise?

Major Neil Thomas, chief C-17A evaluator pilot at McGuire Air Force Base, told us how he strikes a balance. "On the ground and in the air, I evaluate against very clear expectations, but I also have to use judgment in my critique. For example, let's say a pilot lands 11 knots fast—1 knot above the acceptable 10-knot limit by the book. But, in this case, if it doesn't make a practical difference, I can use some judgment," he says.

"But let's take another situation where the rule prohibits a pilot from landing if the tailwind is greater than 10 knots. If he lands in a 20-knot tailwind, I have to fail him, even if he lands perfectly. Why? Because it demonstrates poor judgment and a lack of knowledge of the clear regulations. Ultimately, the outcome is very important, especially in a mission-oriented environment. But, in my evaluations, I'm more focused on critiquing a pilot's process, safety awareness, and judgment than on each perfection or imperfection in the execution."

How does the fetish lead to fingerpointing? Focusing only on results can inadvertently incentivize short-term thinking that jeopardizes long-term goals and interests. After which you'll hear the excuse, "What? I got the results you asked me for. Why are you complaining?"

Sunk Cost Fallacy

Sunk Cost Fallacy refers to our tendency to continue to pursue an effort, in which we've invested irrecoverable time and resources—not because stubbornly pushing forward is the rational thing to do—but because we don't want to feel that our previous efforts were wasteful. In short, sunk cost fallacy makes it hard to cut our losses and walk away from mistakes.

How does sunk cost fallacy show up in business? In *Mavericks at Work*,[14] Taylor and LaBarre describe one way, and it's a phenomenon we've seen many, many times—"companies pursu[ing] dead-end projects long after they should be dead and buried." Why? "Because they load those projects up with financial resources and top-management prestige: Projects become too famous to fail." The investment of ego, reputation, and resources compels leaders and organizations to irrationally "stay the course."

Cliff Dodd, who has served as CIO at several *Fortune 500* companies, invokes a different frame, one that makes stopping the stupidity when it reveals itself to seem like the only sensible thing to do. He says: "I reserve the right to get smarter. And I expect you to do the same."

The idea is to discourage people from stubbornly adhering to a particular process design or decision process. Cliff told us: "If it is not working or it's breaking, just stand up and say, 'You know what? My first decision may have been reasonably correct for what I knew then, but I know a little bit more now so I reserve the right to get a little smarter.'"

He adds: "As a leader in an environment where we're reserving the right to get smarter, we're doing two things. First, I'm holding people accountable to make a decision. And second, I'm also holding people accountable to keep getting better."

Noted author and guru Nassim Taleb holds similar views. "Learn to fail with pride—and do so fast and cleanly," he advises. "Maximize trial and error—by mastering the error part."[15] How do you do that? Taleb is an advocate of "tinkering."

> "Trial and error will save us from ourselves . . . Look at the three big inventions of our time: lasers, computers, and the internet. They were all produced by tinkering and none of them ended up doing what their inventors intended them to do."

At organizations like health care giant Kaiser Permanente, they've integrated "tinkering" into the organization's DNA. They've done this through the use of what they call "unit-based teams," groups of front-line clinicians and other employees trained to use small tests of change to drive continuous improvement through rapid iterations. A unit-based team identifies a challenge, taps the wisdom in the system to identify a potential solution, and then they try it out in a limited way. If it works, they spread it across the organization. If it doesn't, they try something else. No harm, no foul. This approach has led to dozens of measurable improvements in patient and member care while reducing costs and turnaround times

What may be surprising to some is that organized labor is a driving force behind the use of unit-based teams and the "small test of change" methodology. But it makes perfect sense to labor coalition leader John August. "Performance is a labor issue," he contends. And, compared to typical large-scale, too-big-to-fail change efforts, unit-based teams "give people a voice at work, mobilize the ingenuity of the frontlines, and engage workers emotionally and intellectually, giving them a direct line of sight into how they contribute." Which ultimately means more accountability, and less risk of engaging the masses in collective sunk cost fallacy.

An Agile Approach Delivers Results

By Wade Lee

My client, a major publisher with a very conservative, traditional culture, wanted to revolutionize their online presence. We convinced them that instead of taking a "big bang," large-scale approach, we should take an approach that favored low-hype and small wins to build momentum.

First, the team completely redesigned its working environment to accommodate our highly collaborative project. The marketing folks needed to talk to the programming folks, who needed to talk to the business folks. And they all needed access to the project director. To encourage the free flow of ideas and conversation, we literally took down cube walls to bring multiple disciplines into the same space.

The team monitored progress every day in a quick 15-minute stand-up meeting to clearly see our progress as tasks moved toward completion. At the end of each two-week interval, we defined the tasks for the next two-week period, determined ownership, and negotiated realistic completion timelines.

By setting expectations based on what was happening in real-time, we could make tweaks as the project progressed in order to keep our estimates and workloads reasonable.

As the project moved along and we met our milestones, two things happened: We earned more and more latitude from executive management to try new, "non-traditional" things. And the project team gained real grassroots appeal in the organization. By continually driving the vision, building on small successes, and consciously wrapping the experience of the previous steps to fine-tune the master plan, the project produced unprecedented success.

CHAPTER **13**

TREAT MISTAKES AS INTELLECTUAL CAPITAL AND GIVE NEGATIVE FEEDBACK THAT DOESN'T FREAK PEOPLE OUT

There's just one thing that makes it tough to receive negative feedback and learn from mistakes—and that's human nature. As Nassim Taleb writes in *Fooled by Randomness*,[1] humans have a hard time controlling their response to negative information. For example, he says, people who check their stock portfolios once per day, on the whole, make less money than people who check their portfolios once per quarter. Why? Purely as a function of random volatility, the person who checks his or her portfolio more often will have more exposure to negative information. And repeated exposure to negative information is "emotionally draining" and leads to illogical choices.

In recent years, neuroscientists and other researchers have learned lots more about why this is the case. The brain, researchers say, has a "negativity bias." This hypersensitivity to negative information is a survival instinct. It helps people to act fast in response to threats. This is a trait you want in your people much of the time. But not when you are giving them negative performance feedback or trying to help them learn from mistakes. Their brains are wired to process the threat to the ego much the same way it processes a physical threat. One recent study found that "hurt feelings activated the same regions of the brain [that are] activated by broken bones or other physical injuries."[2] In other words, an ego wounded by critical feedback may in some ways *literally* be in pain.

And then what happens in response to the ego "threat" posed by negative feedback? The brain's executive function, which *could* help the feedback recipient rationally process the negative performance feedback and determine how to improve performance, instead stages a walkout. Automatically, the brain's reptile function takes charge. The reptile function is all about speed and survival and—when activated in response to negative performance feedback—compels a defensive response. That response often takes the form of excuse making, a way to protect the ego through "self-serving explanations . . . that aim to reduce personal responsibility."[3,4] What it can sound like is: "Oh, you think I can do a better job of handling customer complaints? Well, I wasn't the one who messed up their service" or "We didn't want to keep that stupid customer anyway" or "Nobody ever trained me right" or "I usually handle them great.

Why are you focusing on this one bad example?" or—you get the idea.

So how do you give negative performance feedback without freaking people out? How do you create an environment where people channel their energy into learning from mistakes instead of covering them up?

One emerging school of thought considers this challenge and says, "Compensate for the brain's negativity bias. The research suggests we are about five times more sensitive to negative information than to positive information. So balance it out. Make sure that positive performance feedback outnumbers negative performance feedback by a 5:1 ratio." It's hard to argue with the data. For example, researchers have found that in the most stable marriages, "[T]here is five times as much positive feeling and interaction between husband and wife as there is negative."[5] More relevant to our discussion, a study of work teams and their performance found that the highest-performing teams "averaged 5.6 positive interactions for every negative one," whereas the 19 lowest-performing teams "racked up a positive-negative ratio of 1:3."[6]

The problem with this approach is in its practical application. How are you supposed to make sure that positive performance feedback outnumbers the negative by a 5:1 ratio? What does that even mean? How are you supposed to keep count? And what happens if you have only one positive thing to say to the person to whom you're giving feedback? What then? Wait until you have four more positive things to share the negative performance feedback? Make four things up? If the goal is to lead conversations grounded in empirical reality, none of these seems like a good choice.

Is there an alternative? We think so.

According to neuroscientists Sandra Aamodt and Sam Wang, a great way to manage emotions is called *reappraisal.* As they explain, "That's when you reconsider the meaning of an event as a way of changing your feelings about it."[7] As such, it involves disciplining the brain's executive function to override the reptilian inclination to freak out and get defensive. Through reappraisal, the executive function does this by reframing the situation.

Here's an example to illustrate how reappraisal works. Our Asia office is in Saigon. It's wild to travel there with Western colleagues who are visiting for the first time. No matter how jetlagged they are, the drive from the airport to downtown rouses them to full consciousness. In Saigon and throughout Vietnam, traffic flows like water, filling all space available. At any point, your taxi may be one of seven vehicles spread across two lanes. Through frequent stops and starts, you're surrounded by other vehicles (scooters, buses, bikes) three inches ahead of you, behind you, and on both sides. And regardless of whether there is a signal or what it displays, your driver will enter intersections without looking for oncoming traffic. Additionally, because traffic moving in your direction is inevitably slow, your driver will take advantage of any open space in the left lane—even if there's a dump truck coming toward you a block away—then slide back into the right lane just in time to avoid a head-on collision.

What's most surprising is that you'll arrive at the office without incident. Sure, you'll pass the occasional fender-bender, but they don't seem to occur with more frequency in Saigon than anywhere else, especially given the traffic volume. What makes this all possible is the horn—and more specifically, honking. Vietnamese drivers honk constantly. If Westerners used horns as much as the Vietnamese do there, we'd have road rage and bloodshed every rush hour. Why? Because we honk our horns and perceive others' honking their horns primarily as an expression of ego and an assertion of relative social power. In Saigon, though, horn honking is a purely functional activity. It just means "I'm *here*." Not "*I'm* here!" And not "Get out of my way! Now! Jerk!"

So, after a few days in Vietnam, visitors reappraise what it means to hear someone honking.

Is it possible to do the same thing in organizations? To promote reappraisal so that communication about mistakes and performance gaps is seen merely as a functional activity instead of an identity threat? So that negative performance feedback isn't experienced *negatively*?

We think the answer is yes because we've seen it happen. In the rest of this chapter we'll highlight some specific strategies for giving your team negative feedback that doesn't freak them out and helping them to treat mistakes as intellectual capital.

Hardcore about Hiring

For starters, the organizations that have the least amount of trouble with negative feedback are hardcore about their hiring. You might be thinking: What do hiring practices have to do with giving negative feedback? If so, we'll answer your question with a question:

Do you have enough confidence in the selection process in your organization that you can assume competence and culture fit for the people you hire? If your people believe that you have confidence in them and want to make them even better, they'll be much more likely to process negative performance feedback the way you'd like them to. However, if they believe that your default assumption is that everyone is a hiring mistake waiting to reveal itself, they'll treat negative performance feedback as an existential threat to their ego and economic security.

Thor Mann, a principal with the management assessment firm ghSMART, illustrates this idea by describing his experience at two different companies. "My former organization describes itself as a feedback-rich environment. But the joke was that everyone is hired 'despite grave reservation,'" he told us. The orientation was, "We didn't really know what we got when we hired you, and whether it will work is anyone's guess."

"And so the feedback at that place was a little more personal—and seemed to be more a message about their lack of confidence in their ability to select the right people and to develop those people rather than anything that I needed to do," Thor says. "And I found that ineffective and merely anxiety provoking."

By contrast, at ghSMART, there is a very strenuous, rigorous process to get hired. And so the orientation around feedback, Thor says, is, "We think you're great. You wouldn't be here if we didn't. And the feedback is going to help you—anything that we can do to help you get even stronger." The focus is on fine-tuning and improvement at the margins.

Hai Le, senior director for Hughes Network Systems in Indonesia, has created the same dynamic on his team. "You can be the smartest person on earth," he says. "But if your attitude is, 'I'm always right. You're always wrong,' we won't hire you." But if you make it through Hai's rigorous selection process, his guiding philosophy is, "We leave no one behind."

"Once we select somebody, it's just like marriage, for bad or good. So when someone's not performing, I'll ask, 'What happened? Because we know you can contribute. Is there something wrong here? Is it personal? Is there a conflict?'" he says. "We're going to do everything we can to push dialogue and solve the problem. When we lose a job or make other mistakes, we ask questions so we can all learn and grow." And because of the "leave no one behind" philosophy, he can count on his team members to participate earnestly in those conversations.

Appeal to Pride and Perspective

Major Neil Thomas is a highly experienced combat pilot who evaluates C-17 pilots for the U.S. Air Force. Before someone can advance from, say, first pilot to aircraft commander, Neil will observe that person for 10 days—typically 14 hours per day.

This means lots and lots of opportunities for negative feedback. But it's not much of an issue, he told us. "I'm dealing with people who've already invested a lot. They've been through intense training, and they want to be there," he says. "Everyone is attentive and trying to get better. So I can be very direct, very specific. They want to get the feedback. I know that if I hesitate or dance around the issue, they'll say, 'Just tell me.'" Because of the pride inherent to the role and perspective that Neil's pilots bring to the cockpit, he doesn't need to worry about dispensing positive to negative feedback at a 5:1 ratio.

Is it possible to promote that kind of pride and perspective in other contexts? Hai Le, to whom we introduced you earlier, has done it with his team. Beside his "leave no one behind" philosophy, Hai is famous for the question he asks everyone he brings on board, "Why are you here?" By encouraging people to frame their experience as career development and pursuit of potential, instead of, say, looking good and collecting the next paycheck, he promotes an environment in which his people are willing, even eager, to learn from their mistakes.

Another Hai Le maxim is also rooted in assumptions of pride and a long-term perspective: "There are so many things that could go wrong, but there's only one thing that can make it right: Building a stronger team," he says. So, when someone makes a mistake, his orientation is don't be embarrassed, and don't hide it. "My goodness!" he'll say, "How are we going to solve it if we don't know about it?"

Another exemplary leader is Walt Buckley, chairman and chief executive officer (CEO) of Internet Capital Group. At the height of the Internet boom, ICG's market capitalization exceeded GM's.

"In the late nineties, every time we made an investment, the stock went up—we could do no wrong," he recalls. "This created a false sense of invincibility. Being in the middle of hypergrowth during the Internet boom was like being in the middle of a tsunami. We were just trying to stay pointed in the right direction. We got so caught up in the success of the moment that we lost a good deal of our discipline and focus. Unless you've been through it before, it's hard to know that you need to seriously look at your organization even when everything is working beyond your wildest dreams."

When the crash eventually came, it hit hard. Instead of blaming everything on forces outside their control (namely, the dot-com crash), Walt led his team in meditating on their mistakes.

"We had to be honest with ourselves about the mistakes we'd made that put us in that place, including the mistakes I made. *What mistake didn't I make?* Looking back, I now call that time the *MEMP period*—Made Every Mistake Possible," he says. "For example, our decision-making process broke down. We had too many people at the table. There was far too little transparency and, as a result, far too little accountability. That was a tough lesson."

But with the tough lessons came an interesting perspective. Think about it: You make every mistake possible, and you're *still* around to fight another day? For a band of warriors, that's a liberating feeling. And with it, Walt created an environment where, without being paralyzed by defensiveness, he and his team could thoughtfully catalog their mistakes, treat them as "intellectual capital," and apply them in their return to battle.

"As we headed up the next hill, we turned every one of those mistakes into a guide for how to climb back up to the top," Walt says.

"Our new emphasis on transparency and discipline required us to move much more deliberately, taking it one step at a time," he told us. "We put the cash flow of our many companies back in order, cleaned up our balance sheet, and moved them to growth. These were the real accomplishments that got us moving again. And today, our decision-making process for investing in companies is very thorough, as thorough as you'll find anywhere."

"And we made it," he adds. "Two hundred transactions later, we bought back all of our debt. It was a very painful, very long process. And the lessons learned were deep, lifelong, and are now an invaluable part of the intellectual capital of our organization."

Empathize

Demonstrating empathy allows the recipient of the negative performance feedback to accept its practical content without accepting the implicit or explicit assertion of your inherent superiority, which tends to trigger a reptile reaction. Tony Conti, an office managing partner at PricewaterhouseCoopers advises, "Where you can, connect what you're asking that person to do with something in the past you've had to work on. Saying, 'I've done the same thing too,' softens the message and shows you empathize."

For similar reasons, he adds that he never expresses criticism or dissatisfaction through e-mail. "I don't deliver bad news in writing because it's there forever." It's got to be a conversation. Why? "When we're counseling someone, we have a tendency to talk more than listen, and as a result, we're not motivating the person to perform," Tony says. "So I've had to learn to lay back, pause, and listen." It's all part of creating the context for feedback in which negative information isn't experienced negatively.

Empty the Boat

There's a famous passage from the Daoist sage Chuang Tzu:

> If a man is crossing a river
> And an empty boat collides with his own skiff,
> Even though he is a bad-tempered man
> He will not become very angry.

But if he sees a man in the boat,
He will shout at him to steer clear.
If the shout is not heard, he will shout again,
And yet again, and begin cursing.
And all because there is somebody in the boat.
Yet if the boat were empty,
He would not be shouting, and not angry.

How do you "empty the boat" in your organization—
and, as a result, take the negativity out of delivering critical
performance feedback? Make feedback exchange a non-
elective activity by building opportunities for it into your
standard operating procedures. For example, if you're
like most organizations and you conduct lessons-learned
sessions (to discuss what worked and what didn't) only after
projects that go badly, the participants (especially the ones
who most need to learn from their mistakes) will show up
with a defensive attitude. However, if "lessons learned" is
just something that you always do, even when a project goes
perfectly, the boat is empty. The same is true if you schedule
and conduct quarterly feedback sessions with all your directs,
regardless of performance—and if those sessions follow a
predictable pattern. There's little perception of agency or
intent. The boat is empty; this is just something predictable
that you do. And, as a result, the brain's negativity bias and
its hypersensitivity to "personal attack" are less likely to
come into play.

Don't Ask Who, Ask Why

Our colleague Binh Nguyen once worked on the management team at the Park Hyatt Saigon. Like most high-end hotels, the Park Hyatt uses mystery guests multiple times each year. No one knows who they are or when they're coming. The goal, of course, is to get feedback on whether staff is delivering the brand according to standards. For example, did the reservation desk pick up the phone in three rings? Did they get checked in within 3.5 minutes of arrival?

When the report arrives later, it compares the mystery guests' experience against 100 brand standards. And what Binh found repeatedly among both management and staff was a tendency to want to try to infer through subtle cues in the data who was to blame for gaps in performance.

Binh recalls, "They'd look at deficits and ask, '*Who* was that?' 'It must have been *this* person? Or *that* person?' But that kind of fingerpointing misses the point. We have a finite amount of time and focus. Better to spend it on determining how to improve the customers' experience or how to improve future training than to supersleuth the report."

Jack Brennan, chairman and former CEO of Vanguard, likely would agree. "A very important part of our culture is the acronym *DAWAW*, which is a term coined by one of the IT [information technology] guys. It stands for 'Don't ask who, ask why,'" he told us. Why is this so important?

"We're always trying to do things better on behalf of our clients. But the way we do that is not by pointing fingers or assessing blame," he says. Instead, it is about asking, "Why aren't we doing as well as we can? Where are the opportunities to improve? And what are the opportunities to capitalize on businesses that we can build?"

As we noted, people use excuses as rapid-deploy defenses of their egos and identities. Accordingly, in an organizational culture in which the default reaction to failure is pointing fingers and assigning blame, it should surprise no one when employees devote their best thinking and finite energy to crafting a narrative that minimizes their responsibility.

By focusing the response to problems and failures predominantly on *why*, not *who*, you can promote a culture in which employees take pride in learning from their mistakes and solving problems.

Dave Watson from the senior team at MedeFinance told us how, as an alternative to the blame game, he approaches performance deficits with a spirit of dispassionate inquiry and a sense of resolve toward solving the problem. "If something's not going well, you don't start by taking out your hammer and clunking people in the forehead. First, ask, 'Okay, we missed a milestone. What's going on? What are the problems? What are the underlying issues?'"

"But it's about taking away excuses, not accepting them," he adds. The idea is to spend some time with them and find a way to solve the problem.

"Blame is nowhere in that conversation," he says. "In a blame game, there's a winner and a loser, and if you're the boss and the other guy is the subordinate, we already know who won. The conversation ended before it started. Instead, just leave it open and say, 'We have a problem that we need to fix, I'm prepared to help, and I can make some suggestions. I'll help all I can.'"

But, he adds, they also need to hear: "You are still accountable. You cannot transfer that back up to me."

Make It Regular

There should never be any surprises in someone's formal year-end review. A surprise is like waiting until after the season is over to tell one of your starters what he's been doing wrong since game 1. It breeds resentment and exacerbates the paranoia and defensiveness associated with negative feedback.

Marshall Goldsmith counsels senior leaders that while their direct reports "seldom want or need coaching to be a time-consuming process," they do very much want "regular 'reality checks' to make sure that they are heading in the right direction." In other words, the "frequency of interaction is often more important than the duration of interaction."[8]

Generously Interpret Motives

One of the things we coach leaders to do is to generously interpret others' *motives* (while confronting the bad *behavior*). An example: You've just learned that Beth, a member of your team, has made a decision about how to staff her project without consulting you first. What's your intuitive read on the situation? Is it: "That's sneaky and disrespectful. She's a problem." Or are you more likely to consider a more generous interpretation of her motives? As in: "Is it possible she doesn't understand that I've got to be consulted in these kinds of situations?"

Keep in mind that we're talking about generosity in your interpretation of Beth's *motives*. This is not about tolerance of her *behavior*. Regardless of where you come down on her motives, you've got to talk to Beth to readjust her expectations and make sure that she understands the consequences of failure to comply. The operative question is: *What are you trying to accomplish?* Get her to confess to operating with bad motives—and, by extension, acknowledge a significant character deficit? Good luck with that. The more you prosecute, the more defensive and indignant she's likely to become. And the accompanying drama is sure to create a gratuitous distraction for everyone around. The other option is to focus on a much more practical goal: Reinforcing your expectations and significantly increasing the odds that Beth's behavior in the future will align with your expectations.

We're not going to prescribe a one-size-fits-every-situation script for going soft on motives, hard on behavior. But the following approach, which you should adapt to fit your natural style and the needs of the situation, works for many:

- *Observation.* "Hey Beth, I see you made a decision about staffing your project without checking in with me first."
- *Hmmm.* "So I'm asking myself: Was I not clear about the requirement? Does she *not* want me to weigh in? Do we have different ideas about what's at stake? So I thought: Instead of wondering, I should come to you directly."
- *Ask a question.* "So here I am. What can you tell me?"
- *Clarify expectations.* "Oh, you didn't know it was a requirement. Yeah, well I'm glad we're having this conversation so that I can clear that up."
- *Confirm understanding.* "Is there anything in the future that might make this requirement difficult to work with? Good. Thanks for this conversation. I suspect we won't need it again."

And then, of course, you've got to hold her accountable.

Lead by Example

Major Neil Thomas, who we introduced earlier, is the chief evaluator at his Air Force base. And while it's his job to evaluate other pilots, if he himself goes 30 days without flying, his next time up is with an instructor—the same as everybody else.

This is a big driver of whether your team will respond to negative information nondefensively: whether you are subject to the same expectations—the same as everybody else. So here's a coaching question to close out this chapter: Are you as a leader modeling and rewarding the behavior you want others to emulate?

1. Do you ask for feedback and then act on it?
2. Do you publicly praise and create instant folklore around people who quickly own up to their mistakes and adopt new ways to make things work?

True Stories

Here are four important things we know about humans and stories:

1. Humans are natural storytellers. We seem to be hardwired to create narratives to explain why things happen and to make sense of our lives.[9]
2. The upside of stories as a means of information sharing is that they are memorable and emotionally engaging. The downside is that, often, they are not very accurate in their depiction of cause and effect. Out of necessity, stories focus on certain details at the expense of others and leave out many relevant facts. Accordingly, the narratives we tell ourselves and each other tend to reflect "deception, blind spots, wishful thinking, the desire to please or manipulate an audience, lapses of memory, [and] confusion."[10]

3. We tend to create stories that are narcissistic and self-serving. We favor narratives that make us look good by putting us, and our unfailingly noble motives, at the center of the action.

4. We also have a powerful tendency to collude with each other to create stories that protect ourselves when mistakes happen. In nuclear power plants, for example, researchers have found that "when people fail, they tend to be candid about what happened for a short period of time, and then they get their stories straight in ways that justify their actions and protect their reputations. And when official stories get straightened out and get repeated, learning stops."[11]

What does this mean to you? It means that when something goes wrong in your organization, your employees, left to their own devices, probably will create narratives to explain the cause and effect of the event, with exculpation (as opposed to accuracy) as their primary objective. And let's be honest: You may very well do the same thing. The problem with creating stories for exculpation is that it makes you and your team vulnerable. If you fail to identify the true cause of what went wrong this time, there's a good chance it's going to come around and kick your butt again and again.

The alternative? One way to lead a conversation grounded in empirical reality and to get a more accurate picture of cause and effect is to engage your team in asking "why" as many as five times. In fact, we believe that being able to conduct a root-cause analysis with your team, at least informally, is a basic leadership competency. Here's an example to illustrate how it works:

One of our clients, the leader of a shared-services organization, found his internal client satisfaction scores declining quarter after quarter. As things got worse, his team began to create and tell themselves stories that pointed the blame at each other, at their leader and his supposed incompetence, and at their idiot clients. These stories offered the people telling them some temporary catharsis but did nothing to solve the problem.

When the leader of the team asked us to help, we encouraged him to lead his team in a root-cause analysis, which we agreed to help structure and facilitate. First, the leader worked with his team to identify in the simplest language possible the top three problems that explained the gap between the satisfaction scores they had and the satisfaction scores they wanted. Then, for each of those problems, they asked "Why?" up to five times.

One of the problems they identified was: We devote too much to projects that are outside our core expertise. And then we don't have enough time to do well the things we're really good at.

The leader asked: "Why do we have this problem?"

The answer (after a few minutes of discussion): "Because we take on projects that are outside our core expertise."

The leader asked: "Why do we have this problem?"

The answer: "Because we don't feel that we have the political power to say 'No' to anything."

The leader asked: "Why do we have this problem?"

The answer: "Because we don't have a clear charter to fall back on. Our department was created because the big-name consulting firm that helped with the last restructuring said we should exist. But they left without helping us determine the scope of our responsibilities— what we should and should not do."

On the one hand, the team felt embarrassed by their epiphany. It was so obvious. How could they not have seen it before? They had been beating themselves and each other up for no reason!

On the other hand, knowing the root cause that they needed to address was liberating. With the help of his boss, his team, and an advisory group comprised of internal clients, the leader created a charter for his department that focused on a finite set of core capabilities highly valued by the people they served. With a clear charter behind them, the team said "Yes" to things they did well and deferred the rest. Internal client satisfaction scores rose modestly the next quarter and shot up the quarter after that.

A few pointers:

- There's nothing magical about asking "why" five times. Sometimes you can identify a suitable root cause after asking "why" only once or twice. If your answers move beyond the practical—for example, life is unfair—you've probably gone too far.
- Sometimes problems have more than one root cause—if this is the case, try to observe the 80/20 rule. If a single root cause explains 80 percent of the problem, focus on it.
- In your discussions, make sure that you can clearly explain the causal relationships. Push your team to answer the question: "Why exactly does this cause that?"
- Make sure that you clearly identify the specific actions you and your team will take to tackle the root causes. Otherwise, what you've created serves merely as a list of excuses.

CONCLUSION

There are three kinds of people. Some people are *saints*—they never make excuses. Some people are *sinners*—they always make excuses. Most people are *save-ables*—give them an excuse, and they'll use it to defend their egos and avoid responsibility. Of course, this excuse making diverts energy and attention away from problem solving and delivering results.

This is why it's so important for leaders to take excuses out of the system by creating the conditions of accountability: Communicating clear and credible expectations. Creating compelling consequences. Leading conversations grounded in empirical reality.

While they're pretty much common sense and easy to remember, the conditions of accountability are not easy to put in place. This is why those who do it well deserve the big bucks and those who don't make excuses for why they can't.

And this is why we wrote this book: To help you lead without excuses, with coaching points based on our research and experience and practical insights from some of the most effective leaders we know. We hope that we've equipped you with at least a few ideas that you can put into practice immediately.

If so, here's what we recommend:

- Identify specifically what you're planning to do to more effectively lead without excuses.
- To help you hold yourself accountable, go to www.lwe.stickK.com (referenced in Chapter 8) and create a commitment contract.

This will help you to translate your good intentions into actual results—and make you a more effective leader at driving accountability and high performance—instead of just talking about it!

NOTES

Introduction

1. Aamodt, S., and Sam Wang. (2008). *Welcome to Your Brain*. New York: Bloomsbury USA.
2. Snyder, C. R., Higgins, R. L., and Stucky, R. J. (1983). *Excuses: Masquerades in Search of Grace*. New York: Wiley.

Chapter 1

1. Darley, John M., and Batson, C. Daniel. (1973). "From Jerusalem to Jericho: A Study of Situational and Dispositional Variables in Helping Behavior." *Journal of Personality and Social Psychology* 100:27.
2. Hanson, Jon D., and Yosifon, David G. (2003–2004). "The Situation: An Introduction to the Situational Character, Critical Realism, Power Economics, and Deep Capture." *University of Pennsylvania Law Review* 152:129.
3. http://en.wikipedia.org/wiki/Rule_of_thumb.
4. Endlich, Lisa. (1999). *Goldman Sachs: Culture of Success*. New York: Alfred A. Knopf, Inc., pp. 18–19.
5. Ibid.
6. Wayne, Leslie. (2009, May 30). "A Promise to Be Ethical in an Era of Immorality." *New York Times*, B1.
7. Rosenbaum, Janet Elise. (2009). "Patient Teenagers? A Comparison of the Sexual Behavior of Virginity Pledgers and Matched Nonpledgers." *Pediatrics* 123(1):e110–e120.

Chapter 2

1. Posner, Richard A. (2009). "How Did This Happen? Why the Economic Crisis Was Not Anticipated." *Chronicle Review of Higher Education* 55(32):B8.

2. Lewis, Michael. (2006). *The Blind Side: Evolution of a Game*. New York: W.W. Norton & Company.
3. Lisa's approach draws heavily on the work of Fernando Flores and Julio Olalla.
4. De Wall, F. (2005). *Our Inner Ape*. New York: Riverhead Books.
5. Here are a couple of additional tips from Alan: "Accountable" is often confused with "responsible" by those unfamiliar with the process. To clarify, ask, "Who approves this?" This is the person with the "A," and we can go so far as to call it "Approval" rather than accountable. Also, some organizations use RASCI, where the "S" stands for "Support."

Chapter 3

1. Heath, C. and Heath, D. (2007). *Made to Stick: Why Some Ideas Survive and Others Die*. New York: Random House.
2. Davenport, T. (2005). *Thinking for a Living: How to Get Better Performances and Results from Knowledge Workers*. Boston: Harvard Business School Press.
3. Guānxi describes the basic dynamic in the complex nature of personalized networks of influence and social relationships and is a central concept in Chinese society.
4. Heath, C. and Heath, D. (2007). *Made to Stick: Why Some Ideas Survive and Others Die*. New York: Random House.
5. Carville, J., and Begala, P. (2003). *Buck Up, Suck Up . . . and Come Back When You Foul Up*. New York: Simon and Schuster.

Chapter 4

1. Simon, H. A. (1971), "Designing Organizations for an Information-Rich World." in Martin Greenberger (ed.), *Computers, Communication, and the Public Interest*, pp. 40–41. Baltimore: Johns Hopkins Press.

Chapter 5

1. Cialdini, Robert B. (1984). *Influence: The Psychology of Persuasion*, p. 167. New York: William Morrow.
2. Ibid., p. 177.
3. Ibid.

Chapter 6

1. Kerr, S. (1975). "On the Folly of Rewarding A while Hoping for B." *Academy of Management Journal* 18:769.

2. Kerr, S. (2009). *Reward Systems: Does Yours Measure Up?* Boston: Harvard Business School Press.
3. http://yglesias.thinkprogress.org/archives/2009/02/baseball_fans_perennially_losing_their_innocence.php.
4. Kerr, S. (2009). *Reward Systems: Does Yours Measure Up?* Boston: Harvard Business School Press.
5. Paumgarten, Nick. "The Death of Kings." *The New Yorker.* 85.14 (18 May 2009): 40–57. Academic Search Complete. Web. 29 May 2009.
6. http://dealbook.blogs.nytimes.com/2009/06/16/goldman-regrets-market-euphoria-that-led-to-crisis/?ref=business
7. Colarusso, Dan. (2009). "Is Goldman Out of Tricks?"; available at www.thedailybeast.com/blogs-and-stories/2009-06-23/is-goldman-out-of-tricks/2/.

Chapter 7

1. Mandler, G. (1982). "The Structure of Value: Accounting for Taste," in M. S. Clarke and S. T. Fiske (eds.), *Affect and Cognition: The Seventeenth Annual Carnegie Symposium on Cognition.* Hillsdale, NJ: Erlbaum.
2. Hsu, Ming, Anen, Cédric, and Quartz, Steven R. (2008). "The Right and the Good: Distributive Justice and Neural Encoding of Equity and Efficiency." *Science* 23(320), Issue 5879:1092–1095.
3. Greene, J., and Baron, J. (2001). "Intuitions About Declining Marginal Utility." *Journal of Behavioral Decision Making* 14:243–255.
4. When talking about changes in utility, economists sometimes refer to *utils* as the unit of conceptual measurement. Given our Kahneman-esque bearings and the fact that it just sounds cooler, we prefer the term *f-points*.
5. Kahneman, D., Knetsch, J. L., and Thaler, R. H. (1991). "The Endowment Effect, Loss Aversion, and Status Quo Bias." *American Economic Review* 5(1):193–206.
6. Eisenberger, N. I., and Lieberman, M. D. (2004). "Why Rejection Hurts: A Common Neural Alarm System for Physical and Social Pain." *Trends in Cognitive Sciences* 8(7):294–300.
7. Cialdini, Robert B. (1984). *Influence: The Psychology of Persuasion,* p. 167. New York: William Morrow.
8. Mochon, D., Norton, M., Ariely, D. (2008). "Getting Off the Hedonic Treadmill, One Step at a Time: The Impact of Regular Religious Practice and Exercise on Well-Being." *Journal of Economic Psychology* 29(5):632–642.

9. Elliot, Mick. (2008, May 17). "UF's Meyer, a Master Motivator." *Tampa Tribune.*

Chapter 8

1. Elliot, Mick. (2008, May 17). "UF's Meyer, a Master Motivator." *Tampa Tribune.*
2. Ellis, A. (2001). *Overcoming Destructive Beliefs, Feelings, and Behaviors: New Directions for Relational Emotive Behavior Therapy.* New York: Prometheus Books.
3. Dubner, S. J., Levitt, S. D. (2005). *Freakonomics: A rogue economist explores the hidden side of everything.* New York: HarperCollins. p. 23.

Chapter 9

1. Conniff, R. (2007). *Ape in the Corner Office: How to Make Friends, Win Fights and Work Smarter by Understanding Human Nature.* New York: Three Rivers Press.
2. *Time Magazine online* (2005, September 19). Available at www.time.com/time/magazine. Retrieved June 28, 2008.
3. Purdum, T. S., and Connelly, M. (2005). "Support for Bush Continues to Drop, Poll Shows." *New York Times online* (September 15). Available at www.nytimes.com/2005/09/15/politics/15poll.html. Retrieved June 28, 2008.

Chapter 10

1. Camerer, C., Loewenstein, G., and Prelec, D. (2005). "Neuroeconomics: How Neuroscience Can Inform Economics." *Journal of Economic Literature* 43:9–64.
2. Klein, G. (2003). *Intuition at Work: Why Developing Your Gut Instincts Will Make You Better at What You Do.* New York: Doubleday Business.
3. Gladwell, M. (2005). *Blink: The Power of Thinking Without Thinking.* Boston: Little, Brown.

Chapter 11

1. American.com/archive/2009/our-epistemological-depression.
2. Paumgarten, Nick. "The Death of Kings." *The New Yorker.* 85.14 (18 May 2009): 40–57.Academic Search Complete. Web. 29 May 2009.
3. Armor, D. A., and Taylor, S. E. (2002). "When Predictions Fail: The Dilemma of Unrealistic Optimism," in T. Gilovich

(ed.), *Heuristics and Biases: The Psychology of Intuitive Judgment*. Cambridge, UK: Cambridge University Press.

4. www.bostonmagazine.com/articles/drew_gilpin_faust_and_ the_incredible_shrinking_harvard/ Drew Gilpin Faust and the Incredible Shrinking Harvard Richard Bradley.

5. Bruch, H., and Ghoshal, S. (2004). *A Bias for Action: How Effective Managers Harness Their Willpower, Achieve Results, and Stop Wasting Time*. Boston: Harvard Business School Press.

6. Ibid., p. 168.

7. http://knowledge.wharton.upenn.edu/article.cfm?articleid=2234.

8. Cohen, Marvin S., Freeman, Jared T., and Thompson, Bryan B. (1995). "Training the Naturalistic Decision Maker." Whitepaper.

9. Weick, K. E., and Sutcliffe, K. M. (2001). *Managing the Unexpected*, San Francisco: Wiley. p. 105.

Chapter 12

1. Forgas, J. P. (1998). "On Being Happy and Mistaken: Mood Effects on the Fundamental Attribution Error." *Journal of Personality and Social Psychology* 75(2):318–331.

2. Tetlock, P. E. (1985). "Accountability—A Social Check on the Fundamental Attribution Error." *Social Psychology Quarterly* 48(3):227–236.

3. Bradley, G. (1978). "Self-Serving Biases in Attribution Process: Re-Examination of Fact or Fiction Question." *Journal of Personality and Social Psychology* 36(1):56–71.

4. Finkelstein, Sydney. (2003). *Why Smart Executives Fail*. New York: Penguin Group.

5. Kersten, E. L. (2005). *The Art of Demotivation*. Austin, TX: Despair, Inc.

6. Paumgarten, Nick. "The Death of Kings." *The New Yorker*. 85.14 (18 May 2009): 40–57. Academic Search Complete. Web. 29 May 2009.

7. http://blogs.reuters.com/davos/save-capitalism-from-the-banks-nassim-taleb/.

8. http://nymag.com/news/businessfinance/56151/index1.html.

9. "Too Close to the Fire: A Problem Few Firefighters Want to Talk About," 2002; available at www.cbsnews.com/stories/ 2002/11/20/60II/main530103.shtml. Retrieved June 26, 2008.

10. "Sleep Deprivation's Rise at Work," BBC News, June 21, 2005. Available at http://news.bbc.co.uk/2/low/uk_news/wales/4114876. stm. Retrieved September 1, 2008.

11. Weir, W. (2006). "Sleep Machismo Hurts." *Hartford Courant*, January 2, p. D.1. Available at http://courant.com. Retrieved September 1, 2008.

12. "Fetish," in *American Heritage Dictionary of the English Language*, 4th ed. Boston: Houghton Mifflin, 2000.
13. Gladwell, Malcolm. (2006). "No Mercy." *New Yorker* Vol. 82 Issue 27, September, 2006, p 37–38. Available at www.newyorker.com/archive/2006/09/04/060904ta_talk_gladwell. Retrieved June 14, 2008.
14. Taylor, W. C., & LaBarre, P. G. (2006). *Mavericks at Work: Why the Most Original Minds in Business Win.* New York: HarperCollins. Page 241.
15. Appleyard, B. (2008, June 1). Nassim Micholas Taleb: the prophet of boom and doom. *The Sunday Times.* Retrieved August 15, 2008, from http://business.timesonline.co.uk/tol/business/economics/article4022091.ece.

Chapter 13

1. Taleb, N. (2005). *Fooled by Randomness.* New York: Random House Trade Paperbacks.
2. Eisenberger, N., Lieberman, M. D., and Williams, K. D. (2003). "Does Rejection Hurt? An fMRI Study of Social Exclusion." *Science* 302(5643):290–292.
3. Markman, K. D., and Tetlock, P. E. (2003). "I Couldn't Have Known: Accountability, Foreseeability and Counterfactual Denials of Responsibility." *British Journal of Social Psychology* 39:313–325.
4. Schlenker, B. R., Pontari, B. A., and Christopher, A. N. (2001). "Excuses and Character: Personal and Social Implications of Excuses." *Personality and Social Psychology Review* 5(1):15–32.
5. Gottman, J. (1995). *Why Marriages Succeed or Fail: And How You Can Make Yours Last*, p. 57. New York: Simon & Schuster.
6. Conniff, R. (2005). *The Ape in the Corner Office: Understanding the Workplace Beast in All of Us.* New York: Crown Business.
7. Aamodt, S., and Wang, S. (2008). *Welcome to Your Brain.* New York: Bloomsbury USA.
8. Goldsmith, M. (2002). "The Six-Question Process." *Insights.* Available at www.marshallgoldsmith.com/articles/article.asp?a_id=87. Retrieved July 14, 2008.
9. Gladwell, M., "Here's why: A sociologist offers an anatomy of explanations," (10 April 2006) *The New Yorker* at: <http://www.newyorker.com/archive/2006/04/10/060410crbo_books> (visited 30 April 2007).
10. Gabriel, Y. (2004). "Narratives, Stories and Texts," in *The SAGE Handbook of Organizational Discourse.* Thousand Oaks, CA: Sage Publications.
11. Weick, K. E., and Sutcliffe, K. M. (2001) *Managing the Unexpected.* San Francisco: Wiley.

INDEX

ABOUT THE AUTHORS

Jeff Grimshaw is a partner in MGStrategy and an expert on accountability. Over two decades, he's helped hundreds of leaders around the globe deliver the results on which they've staked their reputations. He also moonlights at stickK.com as senior advisor, Leadership Solutions, helping leaders apply powerful insights from behavioral economics to improve organizational performance.

With rogue POW/MIA activist Paul Pinkerton, Jeff co-founded Paul's Kids Vietnam Children's Charity, which gives poor, sick, and orphaned children a fighting chance.

He's based in Philadelphia, Pennsylvania. You may contact him at jeff@mgstrat.com.

Gregg Baron, CMC, is president of Success Sciences and an expert in performance improvement. Since 1985 Gregg has been helping leaders create competitive advantage through how their people manage the customer experience at the points of contact. Some of his work includes innovations such as the Communication Coach Simulation Learning System that rapidly facilitates significant improvements in coaching, sales, service, and collections.

He's based in Tampa, Florida. You may contact him at gbaron@success-sciences.com.